GENERATION BLOODLINE
THE SURVIVAL OF LIFE

GENERATION BLOODLINE
THE SURVIVAL OF LIFE

MARY PEARL LAWRENCE

GENERATION BLOODLINE
THE SURVIVAL OF LIFE

Paperback: 978-1-63767-176-4
eBook: 978-1-63767-177-1
Library of Congress Control Number: 2021905618

Ordering Information:

BookTrail Agency
8838 Sleepy Hollow Rd.
Kansas City, MO 64114

Printed in the United States of America

CONTENTS

"THE CHILDREN OF SAM AND ALBERTA RIDLEY IN FULL BLOOM"

God's Grace Mercy   *and Longivity*

THE RIDLEY SOLDIERS
CHARLES FRANKLIN RIDLEY
LEWIS RIDLEY (PICTURED)
SAMMIE LEE RIDLEY (PICTURED)
BLOOMER "UNCLE DOC" RIDLEY
UNCLE LEIGH RIDLEY

LEWIS RIDLEY   **SAMMIE LEE RIDLEY**
                           1918-2006

All of these brave soldiers have gone home to Heaven to be with the Lord Jesus Christ, they were strong courageous men that fought diligently for their country!

WALTER LAWRENCE, JR.
1926-1964
AGE 38
(MARIE RIDLEY – SPOUSE)

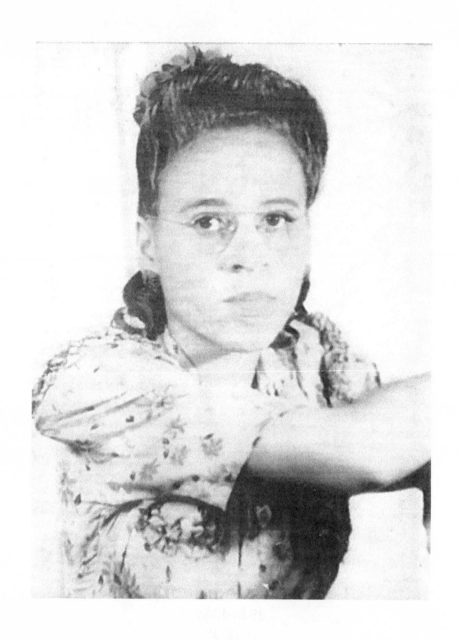

Generations
of
Love

Generations
of
Love

Life on the Come Back Trail
Mary Lawrence

"Music has been a source of great comfort and compassion to me in turbulent and uncertain times. Being back on the entertainment circuit is strangely wonderful and exciting! I love the audience participation, everybody gets to be a part of the act. Hands clapping, toes tapping, let the party begin!"

The moment Mary STEPS onto the stage in her sexy black heels and vintage costumes, this quiet storm erupts into a colorful EXPLOSION of joy and celebration, unforgettable singing and dancing renditions of Tina Turner, Aretha Franklin, Prince and other classic artists.

Please come with me, if you will on the greatest adventure of a lifetime! We'll rescue the lonely hearts from the bowls of despair, recapture that loving feeling and relish in the good old days when life was sweet and oh so mellow!

You can see Mary perform at "The Let's Duet Singing Contest" shows the following venues; Backwoods, Cruisers, Legends, the Grove or The Wishing Well.

Singer-Song Writer
McDonough Talent Signs To Sing Recorders

By MARTHA RINE
Staff Writer

Her attraction to pen and paper and her general attraction as performer may lead to a productive career for Mary Lawrence of McDonough who just recently signed a recording contract with Atlantic City International Records.

Her plans are to record, and hopefully sell a song she wrote herself entitled "What Is Happening What Are The Signs."

"I've always wanted to be a singer but a few years ago I realized my singing career wasn't going too far," she commented.

So she began writing her own songs instead of performing songs for others.

"I have always loved to write but it is harder work than performing," she said.

Miss Lawrence said she has also written several short novels and they have been submitted to a publishing company.

"I can't follow through with the novels though as it takes a lot of money to make the rounds of the publishing houses," she explained as reason for delay in following up that potentially end of her career.

"Right now I plan to stick with writing songs. I mostly compose soul music," added the performer.

In addition to a promising career as a singer-song writer Miss Lawrence recently competed in the Miss Sun's Queen.

"It was one of the greatest experiences of my life," enthused Miss Lawrence about being selected as runner-up for the Queen of the Playpen title.

The contest was sponsored by Sun's Playpen in McDonough, a local night spot.

For coming in second, Miss Lawrence won a trip to Florida. She won a large trophy.

Miss Lawrence lives on Lemmon Street with Marie Lyons.

SHE DID WELL IN PLACING SECOND OVERALL IN LOCAL CONTEST
Mary Lawrence Displays The Trophy In Her McDonough Home

"MY LIFE AND TIMES"

1980-1984
Miss Sonya's Pageant
Record Contract
Newspaper Interview

The eighties was a very critical time in my life when I faced ultimate challenges of being told that I was fat, ugly had too many children and nobody would want to see me compete in a beauty !pageant! Needless to say there was a power and force greater than the negative energy, and this power led me to victory! Not only did I enter and win the Miss Sonya Pageant during this time I was presented with a record contract from Atlantic Records. However, I chose to put all my guarded hopes and dream on hold to raise my three sons who at the time were stair step in age. My decision to raise my son's as a loving and caring single parent was a choice that had to be made, giving my children up for adoption was not an option.!

2014

Fast forward to Twenty fourteen! after all these years of being a loving and caring mother, successfully raising my sons to manhood, I know it's time for me to pick up all my hopes, dreams, and goals off the top shelf and breathe new life into what I know has always been in God's ultimate plan for my life.

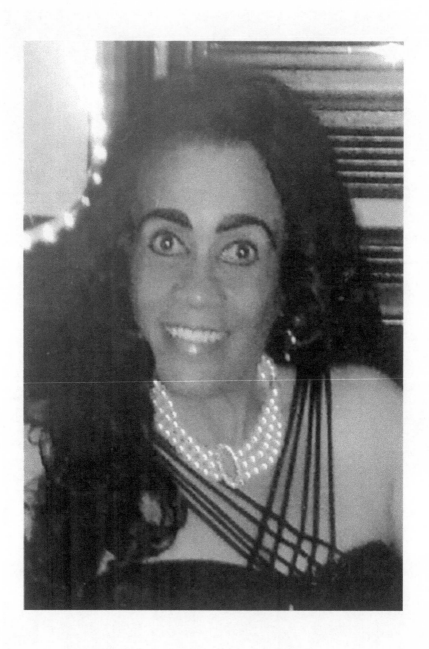

Mary's Quote:
Life is worth living, Live it to the fullest!
And always wear a smile!

Mary P. Lawrence

Mary Lawrence At Photo Shoot

ABOUT THE BOOK

Generations is about three generations of strong black (mulatto) women with caucassion characteristics and ancestry. They were not accepted by black or white society. Their silky light skin and long beautiful black hair shined brilliantly as golden candles covered in precious diamonds and priceless jewels atop the great Liberace's flamboyant and extravagant pianos and sparkling costumes! Yet, as breathtakingly alluring as these living portraits were, there lurked a haunting curse of perilous doom and uncertainty! These brave women had true gut determination win a scorching battle that poured smoldering coils of seering pain and agony deeply into their bleeding hearts, as they mourned the great tragedies of life's never ending turmoils! Their magnificent beauty fanned the flames of wicked, delicious aromas! Intoxicating perfumes filled their nostrils with unquenchable thirsts for the outer-limits of hot blazing passion fires that burned! Burned! And Burn!

1845-1855- Laura Mariah was a five year old slave child when she entered the Revel family home. A full grown woman with child, at fifteen, she exited the back door with a broken heart! Her baby was snatched from her loving and nurturing arms just after birth and laid into the busom of her master's barren wife, Victoria!

Thomas Revel, was a very rich and powerful businessman. A handsome rouge with much swagger in his steps! So charismatic, all eyes turned toward his direction whenever he entered a room! Hot sexy and very irresistible to the many feminine conquest of his day! He and his doting wife resided in a grand southern style antebellum mansion, that was decorated with lavish silk and satin draperies, exquisite hand made furnishing with notable carving designs, imported all the way from New England and Spain!

1855- Laura Mariah had grown up to be a very pretty young girl! Her pigtail plats were so long, they draped all the way down to her tiny waist and voluptuous hips! Thomas, obsessed with Mariah, scenting all around her like a dog in heat, followed her every movement! One chomping bite into her insatiable forbidden fruit became an irresistible delicacy to his hungry lips, rendering him as helpless as a new born infant suckling nourishment from its mother's swollen breasts! The juicy nectars flowed potent and fast, from man to woman, until, a new life was conceived! Seconds after little Samuel was born, his father, Thomas snatched him from Laura's grasping embrace, cleaned him up with pure spring water from a nearby basin, wrapped him up in a soft blue blanket, then carried him to his wife Victoria, who was bed reddened, stricken with grief from the loss of their stillborn son! Holding him so tightly to her chest, she thanked God for the tiny little miracle bundle of life!! At last, Thomas Revel had his first born son, named Samuel!!!!

1857-- Thomas, before sending Laura Mariah farther south to work in the sugar can fields, warned her that if she told anyone that she was Samuel's mother, she and Samuel would be killed!

Laura settled into her new home as best as she could. She met a fine looking buck with a strong back and fearce temper! They lived in the same slave quarters, a two room shack with dirt floors. Buck became jealous whenever any of the other men in the camp spoke kindly to Laura. While working in the cane field, he got so mad, in a jealous rage he swung his sharpened blade hard across the lower part of Laura's arm, slicing it right down to the bone! Blood flowed profusely from the gaping wound, saturating her clothes with the rich red life fluids as she fell to the ground screaming in horror and disbelief that this man could be so cruel and evil!! Speaking incoherently in a foreign tongue, the heavenly language between her and her god, she begged The Lord above to spare her life and give her the power to overcome this senseless and brutal assault!

The other women in the quarters, came to Laura's side. They administered aide to her by tying a cloth tight around her injured arm, then carried her back to the cabin where they applied homade salves and herb tonics to help her get back up on her feet.

However, not being able to care for herself, Laura Mariah stayed with that evil man, even after they both were freed from slavery! They moved back to Flovilla Ga in the negro section of the town. Several years later Buck died, leaving Laura Mariah to fend for herself. She found work as a babysitter for the other women's children, who worked as maids and housekeepers in Atlanta.

1914-1915-- Grandma (momee) Alberta was a big tall strong woman with a stout frame that was good for child bearing. She met Grandpa Sam at a livestock sale barn auction. She was delivering food and refreshments to Ms. Higgins's brothers who also attended the sale. Alberta was Ms. Higgins's care giver and companion. She had been living with the Higgins family since she was 12 years old. Ms. Higgins was an elderly obese lady, so fat that she could not bend over to tie her shoes. A big old wind bag with large pink cheeks that shook every time she bellowed her over bearing commands to Alberta. If Alberta made an error when performing any of her many chores, old Lady Higgins would pluck her on the head with a whipping stick. Alberta washed clothes, dishes, swept floors, cooked five course meals, cut out patterns from discarded newspapers and made clothes for herself and Ms. Higgins, helped Ms Higgins with personal grooming, bathing, combing hair, cutting toe nails, planted a vegetable garden, tended the flowers, and made minor house repairs.

1917-- Sam and Alberta were united in holly matrimony. Between the two of them, they raised 14 children. However, little Lucille, died at five years of age. The other children's names were; Ruby, Doc Blummer, Sarah, Julia, Tassie, Sammie Lee, Charles Franklin, Laura, Lige, Obie, Marie, Evelyn and Lewis.

1924-Samuel found out the truth about his real mother Laura Mariah and located her living in a shanty house outside of Jackson. In frail health, eyesight nearly gone, this stubborn old woman held on to her faith that one day before she died, she would once again hold her lost son Samuel close to her heart! Hearing the door of her humble home slowly open, and someone calling her name Laura! Laura Mariah! Yes, she boldly replied. Do you know someone named Samuel, he asked. Samuel! My son, I have waited so very long to hear your voice!!! She said. In tears of joy, the two of them embraced each other for a very long time!!! Then Samuel carted up his mothers keepsake items and brought her home to live with him and his family until her death a few years later!

1929-- Grandma Alberta and her children saved the family home from the great fire. She was acting like a general commanding her kids to fall into position, forming a line from the well to the back side of the house, drawing the water and passing it bucket after bucket back to the latter where she was waiting up on the roof dousing the flames.

1939-- The girls snuck out of the house and went to Mr. Bubbas Juke Joint. Left behind, little Evelyn spilled the beans to Grandma Alberta, and boy, was she hoping mad!! She heard Tassie and her sisters coming up the road snapping their fingers, giggling and talking about the good time they had had dancing the truck dance and Susie Q and jitterbugging with the fellows. Tassie, started singing the blues song How Long, Baby How Long? Hiding in the bedroom closet with strap in hand, as the girls snucked back in and nestled underneath the covers, Grandma Alberta burst through the door and started whipping behinds left and right. She really beat down on Tassie for singing those evil jezzebel blues! With sore bottoms, all the girls set on the front pews of the church during Sunday morning service. Tassie sang them good old gospel songs with the senior choir!

1941-1946-- All five of Grandma Alberta's sons were drafted into the military. Every available young man was taken from his family and sent to Basic Training Camp where he received combat procedures and survival skills on foreign land. They learned how to shoot fire arms, drive army tanks, throw hand grenades and jump out of air planes.

Alberta's sons Sammie Lee, Charles Franklin, Doc Blummer, Lewis and Lige were members of all black, African American infantry units. All these brave soldiers of strength and courage fought diligently with great pride and honor! They served their mandatory tours of duty across the seas to Belgium France, D day at Normandy, and Germany.

Sister Marie's assignment was to write each of her brothers every week as dictated by momee Alberta. She would always instruct Marie to close each letter with "Son, keep your head down low, and remember your maker, Jesus Christ! Your heavenly father will surely bring you back home safe and sound into your mother's loving arms!" Then she and Marie carefully seal the envelopes, attach proper postage and place them inside the mail box standing near the entryway of the house.

1944-Uncle Charley Frank was brave, liked to try new things. He was very smart, taught himself how to play the piano and guitar from music lessons he ordered in the mail. He was a lively character with a strong wit and sharp tongue, slick black hair that he liked to flip back and forth and dance like Cab Calloway. He told great war stories! During his tour of duty in Belgium France and D Day At Normandy, it was a cold winter morning, fridged waters lapped on each side of the vessel that he and his comrads sailed upon. With eyes wide opened, anticipation and fear danced in their pounding hearts as they swallowed back screams of dooming panic and terror!!! It was there that he met and lost the love of his life, a red headed beauty named Frenchy! Distraught and inconsolable from his great loss, three weeks later, he was rescued from his great depression by a gentle man, with a gentle touch. This lovely man nourished him, mind, body and soul back to health.

1946- Grandma Alberta's prayers were once again answered! All five of her brave sons, with every limb intact, came marching home! Charles, however, came back with a sad and lonely heart! And also a secret about the gentle man with the gentle touch!!! He carried this secret for many years and only revealed it to his older brother while on his death bed!!

1947-- Marie, my mother, and grand daughter of Laura Mariah suffered the taunts and slanders and physical abuse from the other women in Dark Town. They envied her long thick black curly hair and silky pale skin. They were mad as hell when she married my father Big Daddio as he was so fondly called. He had just returned home after serving in the Navy and was ready to spin his heals on the dance floor. With some military benefits, he was considered a good catch. Panda, an evil voo doo priestest, attempted to set Marie on fire in the cotton fields!

1963

Even though Walter had served in the military, because of racial hatred and prejudice, the only job he could find at the time was on a garbage truck in Atlanta Georgia. Money was tight and scarce. There were a lot of mouthes to feed. Marie had a big family, 10 kids to be exact. Father owed a lot of white merchants in the small town and didn't back down when confronted with over due bills. He had gotten into a shoving match with a grocer about money owed for food supplies. There was also talk going around that he was married to a white woman! Years later it was rumored that a deadly plot had been hatched to kill him and place his body on the rail road to cover up the dasterly deed! Mother, not knowing the alledged truth, hated and blamed the rail road for father's death.! Her words were filled with so much sadness and great loss! "You never know how something so innocent as an old whistling train chugging down the tracks, woke us up as children making sure we got up on time to get ready for school, would become a vessel of sudden death!! Screeching wheels scrubbing against metal rails came in here and snatched away my husband's last breath of life on this earth!!! Why! Why! Why!!"

1964--Marie and some of the older kids worked in the cotton and butter bean fields to make ends meet, while Walt Jr. worked on Mr. Bass's farm as a field hand. It was there that he overheard a group of men talking in the barn, bragging about how they had murdered his father and placed his body on the railroad tracks! Fearing for his remaining family's safety, he kept the awful secret of what he had overheard to himself for many years until after all his brothers and sisters were grown.

1969-- Mary, Marie's Daughter survived childhood rape, physical abuse, mental anguish and torcher from individuals whom she had loved and trusted! Black girl! White Girl! We don't want you here! Go back where you belong! These were childhood taunts Mary endured thru her years in school by some of her class mates. She survived a loveless marriage full of hate and scenting of death! Her Husband, Daren was a vicious tyrant who beat her unmercilessly many times! So severe that she was only inches away from death's door! She was not allowed to walk with her head up, rather, to cowar with her eyes stareing down at the ground underneath her feet!

1975--The final tragedy involved her brother, or should I say sister, yes he was gay. He was big and bold, walked hard, slammed doors, always wanted to be the center of attention, and to hear him tell it, he was the most beautiful barby doll that ever walked the face of the earth! Whenever he danced, he would hit the floor hard with his hands, then come back up twisting and twirling like a majorette!! Mary could not understand why he hated her so much! Before he went to Atlanta, they use to hang out and party! There were times when she use to give him money to buy beer and cigarettes. And now, every time you turned a corner, he was torchering her children in order to provoke a fight which resulted in her and her children getting thrown out of the house, sometimes sleeping in her beat up old station wagon or under the stars and dark night skies! David sought after every male aquaintance of his sister, Mary. No man was off limits, not even her husband Daren!

1985-- Bloody gore and mahem transformed a happy occasion, her birthday into a unforgettable nightmare with far reaching consequences! Separated from her children, behind steal bars, she fell on her knees and called on her heavenly father to be victorious over her unfortunate plight! Satan surrounded her with his all his she deviled henchmen as she tossed and turned endlessly on the hard bunk bed in her cell while listening to the moans and groans of intimate pleasures of the other inmates. These girls acted like men in every fashion! Kissing and caressing each other so passionately, they exchanged cards and roses on Valentine Day! Upon her Experience the betrayal of her mean selfish husband Daron, who was in denial of his homosexual desires! If he had only been forth coming with these feelings, maybe they could have ended the relationship on far better terms! Meet her jealous deceitful brother, David, who thought he was the most beautiful and gorgeous one, more feminine and sexual than any real woman on earth!

Say hello to her new friends, the party girls, Mary Anne and Betty Boo! Seeing Mary as a lost soul bound by an intimidating fear that rendered her a shy shrinking violet, the girls knew she desperately needed help to shake loose and let her hair down! Their wild antics and sexual prowess was so dam good that they quickly seduced and corrupted her with its boldness that catapulted Mary into irresistible realms of forbidden desires, giving all to raw emotions and denying nothing to her unbridled flesh!!!

Witness her most miraculous feat yet, the transformation from a scared, shy child of darkness to a woman of positive light, pure joy and inspiration!! See how she became a saintly grandma figure to so many little angel faces at the River Wood Projects Hood! How she provided after school meals and shelter from the rain for the kids until their parents came home! She gave Little Eddie and little Desmond their first job! They earned 50 cents each every time they carried her trash to the dumpster!

"Yeah, I have a story to tell! It's a story of how I over came all those evil she devils and he devil henchmen of St Lucifer, himself, who tried to destroy me with constant mockery, ridicule and slanderous insults! You too old! Look at all those kids you got! Honey, nobody wants you! You fat ugly slut! You can't sing your way out of a paper bag! HA! HA! HA! Isn't it so funny, dirty and low down, how the devil uses those closest to your heart to hurt you the most!!

I felt like I lived in a fish bowl! If I went to my car to get away from my evil brothers in crime, (AKA) Artlena and Roschetta, would peer at me from behind the kitchen curtains, if I went to sing karaoke, they would lie and say I went to meet some dude! IT got so bad that I slept on the floor, in my car, had to slip around in my mother's kitchen to pilfer for food while they were asleep or gone out of the house!

Then one day, I picked up a bible and started reading it! Instantly, all those painful memories fell off my shoulders!! Those shackling chains that once had me captive to my past no longer had any power over me, I was free!! And whom the son sets free is free indeed! I have found a friend that sticks closer than any sister or brother! I found peace, joy and love! I found Jesus Christ!! Amen! Amen! And Amen!!"

WHY MISS MARY WROTE THIS BOOK

This is a true story about me and my family, a compelling drama about three generations of America's rejected children, the mulatto progeny of antebellum slaves. In these modern times, we may be referred to as bi-racial children. These women shed blood, sweat and tears to survive the crippling poverty stricken hardships of the cold bitter south! They waged a strategic battle to secure ultimate victory over a society that had no sympathy for its bastard offspring! The price they paid for acceptance was way too high!!

I am writing this book as a means of healing and relieving the suffering of other people just like me who may be involved in a violent relationship, struggling with their own identity and thinking of committing suicide as I once contemplated!

As a bi-racial child, I was not accepted by black or white society! I didn't understand myself until I discovered the profound significance of my genetic history.

My father was allegedly murdered by a racist mob who thought that he was married to a white woman. My siblings and I worked in the cotton fields to keep food on the table! My mother took in ironing to provide a roof over our heads. We all lived in a five room shack with no inside bathroom or running water.

I was raped by two teenage hoodlums when I was only twelve years old, while attending middle school, I was taunted with racial slurs by my fellow classmates. My nick names were white girl, black girl and half breed! These words of cruelty weighed heavily upon my heart! Surrounded by hundreds of students and teachers, I felt so very alone!

I survived violent drug infested affairs with evil and possessive men that once promised to love, honor and cherish me forever! I lived in a horrible nightmare from the bottomless pits of hell on earth! Embedded in a disparaging time of restless anguish and torment, wondering why my life was marred by so many unfortunate circumstances??

"Why am I called white girl? No friend to even words! The blood in my veins wars against my spirit, pulling me in all directions until I am dizzy with confusion! I am a slave to the indignant convictions of man! A runaway in bondage until my inward soul is free! Who am I? Oh where do I belong??

White girl! Black girl! We don't want you here! Go back where you belong! These childhood taunts kindled with splinters of diabolical hate and intimidation are worrisome burdens of agony that weigh heavily upon my mind, body, and soul!

What manner is my brother to say he is my brother, then, lock the doors of comfort and drive me into the dark night? Must I bear the cross that leads to the land of the lost? Oh where will I find refuge in this perilous plight??

The pain in my heart pierces the very core of my being! I cry in desperation for flesh and blood, yet, self denial controls! Loving affection fade from my sight! My soul lingers to an imitation of love portrayed in mocary of a funeral forcade!

Compassion as gently as it caresses, in terror and disbelief does not see me, yet, warns to reality that it must flee me! Fate paints a haunting portrait of rejection, excruciating pain that rips my emotions to swreds!

Though suptrafuse never slumbers nor sleep, I will never fear it! For death is but an adoration of relief, a welcomed rest from torment and grief!

The answer to my destiny must inevitably lye in the equation of my ancestral components. This theory was the catalyst that set to blaze an intense desire to discover who I am, and, where do I belong???

My quest led me to an intriguing oldster who lived in Flovilla Georgia. Set in her ways, she was an onnery as a howling dog and spat out words of vermin profanity like a drunken sailor. Known throughout the town as a witch doctor, Miss Dida stored every herbal remedy imaginable to treat all k

SPECIAL DEDICATION TO:
T.W.

Thank you very much for all the wonderful memories we shared during some difficult times.

There we were down in the country, held up in a little shack with no lights or running water, it was so cold that you could see our frosty breathe as we exhaled the cold wind.

I remember you sitting on the bench in front of your granny's old upright piano and your fingers began to dazzle the keys with a soft sweet melody called, "Misty!"

You had a big grin that covered your face as you watched me settle into a mellow mood and I began to dance like I was in a scene from an old Hollywood movie! Then we raised our glasses of plum granny wine and toasted to some better times ahead! You will be forever remembered. Thank you again Mary.

SPECIAL DEDICATION!

TO ALL SINGLE MOTHERS AND VICTIMS OF DOMESTIC VIOLENCE

Ms. Mary wants you to know that you are SOMEBODY! You MATTER! You have the right to be loved and honored by your significant other! If you are being physically and mentally abused by your loved one, run away as fast as you can from this monster in disguise! Lying lips that say I love you in one breath, then, call you bitches and hoes in another breath and throw punches and kicks you with fists and feet during attacks of violent altercations, leads one to believe that a person of this character is deadly and dangerous to you and himself, is insecure and have low self esteem issues! If he hits you once, he will hit you again!

Ms. Mary wants you to know That God made you perfect in every way! Man's negative words do not define who you are!! God designed and created your spirit with seeds of greatness, destiny and purpose for such a time as these! Be a beacon of light to a dying world and those lost souls who walk in darkness! Inspire them to hold on to the hope and belief that tomorrow will be a better day! You are a priceless portrait of the master's piece, etched in grace and tender mercy by your heavenly father, almighty God! The strife of life has made you strong, victorious and overcomers from adversity to beautiful flowers of success in full bloom! Be who God made you to be, live your dreams, boldly stand and shine as the most beautiful twinkling stars in the skies! Trust and believe that what God gave you even before your birth, man cannot take it away! Amen! Amen! Amen!

PROLOGUE

Laura Mariah, Momee Alberta, Mariah Marie and Mary, searched their subconscious minds of self awareness, an inward mental journey to find ever elusive true love and happiness! Their quest was captured by a heartless fate that bombarded their lives with tears of sadness, for uncertain splender faded with the passage of time! Their venture of sensual erotica to siege the elixor of living ecstasy and transform their desolate hearts into rejuvenated flowers of desires had taken a tole on their mind, body and spirits!!! Their beauty was a curse that haunted them relentlessly! There was no where to run or hide from the nightmare of hell on earth!!!

Their magnificent beauty fanned the flames of wicked, delicious delicacies! The scents filled their nostrils with unquenchable aromas and ravenous appetites to the outer-limits of hot blazing passion fires that burn! Burn! Burn!

Existing in the twilight of neutrality, they were doomed to sail an endless voyage as castaways, swept overboard by lies, violent rages, sexual abuse and death as they struggled to survive while mending their broken hearts!

Chapter 1

A Few Simple Questions

My story starts like this . . . I've always had a few simple questions of which the answers will be significant to my very existence. "Why am I called 'white girl'? No friend to even words! The blood in my veins war against my spirit. Pulling me in all directions until I am dizzy with confusion! I am a slave to the indignant convictions of man! A runaway in bondage until my inward should be free! Who am I? Where do | belong?" Marie's daughter Mary was unlucky in love and always picked the wrong man to share her life! She was devastated and heart-broken over the last relationship that ended in violent and assaults that destroyed her world!

My quest led me to an intriguing oldster, who lived in Flovilla, GA. Set in her ways, she was as ornery as a howling dog and spat out words of vile profanity like a drunken sailor. She was known throughout the town as a witch doctor. Miss Dida knew every herbal remedy imaginable to treat all kinds of ailments from A - Z. Her wicked laugh would chill your bones! The scent of blood and death lurking through her voice was also evident in her hallow and demonic eyes!

Miss Dida wouldn't unleash any of her secrets unless I shared her food. While roasting peanuts in an opened fireplace and preparing desert cakes from her homemade jams and jellies; she began to let all the skeletons out of the closet!

I was reluctant to sample her unsightly entrees. However, I realized that I must doggishly devour these tarts in order to gain her confidence and release the hidden secrets of my ancestors.

Motioning for me to hand her stuff cup from the mantle, she packed her lower lip full of contents. The flames blazed intensely as she spat into the burning logs. Fear gripped my heart. Stopping me in my tracks as her eyes turned crimson red!

"You're Rye's daughter aint yah?" She asked. "The spirit told me you were coming! No reason for you to fear ole Miss Dida. You be blood of my blood" she assured. "I will not harm you. Come closer by my side, and I will tell you what you want to know" she declared.

With her calming words, I slowly knelt by her side on the floor of her humble yet strange abode. I listened with an attentive ear to her chilling recollections! Tinkling chimes rang out in the blistering air as she spun an evil tail of terror, pain and death! For a moment, it seems as if though the winds leaped into the fireplace and danced with the burning flames! Flying objects began sailing across the room in a waltzing fashion. My heart beat fast. Ina a panic, I began gasping for a breath of fresh air! I wanted to run and hide but fear rendered me motionless and held me captive as she transformed into a ghostly hostess!

She uttered, "Come closer my sweet child and I will tell you the story of anger eyes that roam the skies with blood dripping tears! Let's travel back to yester-years to discover the truth of life and death. I will unveil the torturous secrets long buried in the silent gave of time!"

CHAPTER 2

GREAT GRANDMA LAURA MARIAH HOW IT ALL BEGAN

The rain fell in ice cold showers as thunderous bolts of lightning lit up the night skies. In pitch black darkness, guided by a hanging lantern and a snapping whip, you could hear the huffs of the horses trotting down the muddy roads. Laura Mariah, a five year old slave child sat in back the buggy driven by one of the Revelle family slaves. The rain blanketing the tears trickling down her saddened face. Laura had big beautiful eyes and a head full of curly long pigtails. Her dark chocolate skin glistened in the rain. The memory of being torn from her mother's caring arms at a local slave and traders sale burned deeply within her aching heart. Watching in horror at the white bidders with dollar bills clinched tightly in their fist, she prayed that whoever bought her mother would buy her as well. Her worst fears came true on this stormy night, when a fat stinking, cigar puffing brute of a man purchased her mother. He refused to buy Laura. He thought that her mother would not have time to care for her. She needed to be able to do many chores and care for his ailing wife and family.

Holding on tightly to a piece of embroidery ripped from her Mother's tattered apron, frightened and alone, she stood still as a lifeless statue with the remaining slaves to be auctioned at the sale.

Tom Revelle, a local farmer and businessman noticed Laura's frail body shivering wet from the pouring rain. His mind began to wonder about his own daughter at home and decided to buy her as a companion for little Ashley.

Ashley was an only child. Without any real brothers and sisters to play with, she often created imaginary characters to fill the empty void in her life. Her hair was yellow and bright as the sunlight, and her giggly laughter made one smile just listening to all those amusing tones. She loved to have tea parties, play hide and seek games, and dress up in her mother's pretty hats and dresses and a string of pearls around her neck. She would look in the mirror and say, "I do declare I am just about the prettiest little thing in all of Jackson, Georgia! Oh dear sister Jenny, don't you agree?"

Her mother worried that her games of pretense was getting out of hand. Ashley wouldn't eat breakfast or dinner unless a place setting was on the table for her fantasy playmates. She would carry on a conversation with them all during supper.

Ashley was so pleased to see Laura coming inside the large doors of their home. She was accepted as part of the family. The two children ran about the house laughing so gaily and freely up and down the stairs. Ashly taught Laura how to read in secret while hiding in her bedroom closet. With candle light view, she would listen as Laura read from school text books. She often corrected any mispronunciation of words.

Several years later, Mrs. Revelle decided to send Ashley to an all girl boarding school. Laura remained with the family as a cook and helper. Ashely was puzzled and didn't understand why her mother w: sending her so far away.

The Revelles' lived in a large two story mansion resting on fifty acres of rich and fertile land. The roonid were colossal with tall ceilings and lengthy windows. The study sat across from the grand ballroom where the family held lavish dinner parties while discussing politics of that era. The women often adjourned to the parlor leaving their counterparts to themselves after dinner. There were lively conversations about the latest fashions and perfumes from France. They were all proud to show off their new earrings and necklaces and diamond rings. Maybe even share a few delicious recipes.

Laura Mariah's room was dimly lit by a smokey globed kerosene lamp that cast shadows about the walls. Adorning the mantle over the fireplace were keepsakes. The wind was strong as it blew through the cracks of the floor, lifting the flames from the burning logs. Still a bit frosty inside, she hovered underneath a warm quilt that she and Ashley had made together sometimes back in the spring. Laura thought of Ashley everyday. She hoped and prayed that she was alright. The Revelle's were entertaining guest that evening. Laura could hear all the people talking and laughing in the parlor. Maybe they'll leave some of those nice finger sandwiches and peppermints. I'll be more than happy to scoop some up in my nap sack and go for a nice long walk in the woods she thought.

During the mid eighteen hundreds, having a large number of slaves was a statement of wealth. Tom Revelle owned nearly two hundred human beings. They were quartered in small shacks a good distance away from his fashionable estate. The stalls were stocked with grand stallions; bucks used as breeds to increase his valuable herd.

Mr. and Mrs. Revelle lived in a lavish southern styled mansion located in South Jasper County. Their home was surrounded by peach orchards and plush gardens. The sun cast a rainbow of beautiful colors as it peered through the large oval windows of this angelic monument. From the top of the balcony, one could view the plantation for miles around. The wide corridors were adorned with family portraits. The windows were decorated with lavish silk and satin draperies. Exquisite hand made furnishings with notable carving designs all the way from Spain and New England.

Tom Revelle was a powerful frontiersman. He was one of the richest men in South Georgia. Toasted as a loving father and husband, but behind this Cloak of prestigious endeavors of honor and respectability, lurked a savage beast. He was a handsome rouge with a roving eye for the bizarre. His alluring and adoring personality could melt any barriers of resistance. With much swagger in his steps, he had an air of distinction and fascinating intrigue. So charismatic that all eyes followed his every direction. He was hot, sexy and irresistible to all feminine conquests of his day.

Poor Mrs. Revelle was a frail delicate woman. Her hair was as yellow as corn silk and her voice was as soft as rose petals. She was committed to the man in her life and loyal to the bone. No matter the price she had to pay. She and her husband Tom were widely acclaimed in all social circles.

Laura had no knowledge of the whereabouts of her biological family. So she considered the Revelle's as her family. She mastered the art of cooking at a young age. She could turn mere scraps from the table into delicious meals. Among her favorite dishes were, chitterlings, hog maws, pig ears and feet, pork brains stew, beef liver with onion gravy, corn bread, and fried chicken with corn fritters. One could smell the sweet vanilla aromas from her cakes for miles as it drifted in the cool breeze. Her biscuits were so fluffy they melted in your mouth. All the neighborhood kids loved her famous tea cakes with cinnamon on the crusts.

Rising up early in the morning, Laura milked the cows for fresh milk to prepare a hearty breakfast for the family. Humming gaily as she went about her daily chores, gathering eggs from the hen house, sweeping the yards with a homemade brush broom made of small tree branches, watering the garden, and drawing water from the well. After doing chores she would hurry upstairs to fill Mrs Revelle's bath tub with lavender bath salts and hot water heated on the stove.

On laundry day she and the other workers brought bed linens, towels, and other garments outside and placed them on a cart like table. In a big round iron pot, Laura prepared to wash clothes. Placing two large garments at a time into a wash tub with rubbing board. She commenced to scrubbing each piece on the boarding sousing it down back and forth into the water until it was fresh and clean. It took a half day to complete the washing cycle.

Years had been very kind to Laura, like the good book says, her clothes had not grown old and still fit her well. Each day she became more and more beautiful. Her cheerful singing rang out from the kitchen as she stirred in the pots of food. She would always sample the pots to make sure she had just enough seasonings to give her succulent dishes that magical flavor.

Laura wondered why Master Tom began dining in the kitchen. With fire in his hungry eyes, he watched her as she prepared the family meal. There was a secret attraction for her that would eventually unfold.

Separated from the other slaves, she grew lonesome and tired. She often longed to see her birth mother.

Mrs. Revelle was devoted to Laura as a child, they comforted each other. Their lives were filled with joy and laughter. All of that would soon change. As Laura matured, the Mrs. began pushing her away. Laura never thought that a woman she had loved so dearly as a mother, would become a distant shadow.

Mrs. Revelle felt sometimes less than a woman. The most precious gift of a son heir to her beloved husband, was not in her possession to give. After having Ashley, Victoria Revelle miscarried twice and could not carry anymore babies to full term. The third attempt failed, and left her severely ravaged body in a barren state.

Thomas had become obsessed with Laura. He followed her every move. He tracked her like a dog i. heat. One beautiful morning, Tom was once again in the kitchen admiring Laura as she prepared breakfast. Her long pigtails touched her buttocks and swayed about her waist as she stirred the pots on the six eyed wood burning stove. Tom's penis swelled to its maximum capacity and exploded inside of his trousers! He became embarrassed when Laura caught a glimpse of him standing behind her and quickly exited the door.

Later that same afternoon, the butler instructed her to sleep in the barn. Without questioning his orders she obeyed. That night she laid on a comfortable pile of hay. She imagined herself nestled on a bed of feathers and drifted into clouds of peaceful sleep. In her dreams she saw herself as a mistress of a grand and luxurious mansion. Her servants waited on her hand and foot obeying her every command. She was dressed so eloquently in a beautiful evening gown with matching sparkling necklace and earrings! Shiny gold candelabras decorated the dinner table along with fine white linen tablecloths and sterling silverware. She asked herself . . . Am I dreaming? Oh Please Dear Lord let this be real! I am a free woman! I can go where ever I want! Whenever I want!

Awakening from loud thunder, Laura was startled to see her Master's silhouette standing only a few feet away. He was on a desperate quest to ease the turbulent roar of sexual gratification that chiseled at his aching bones. The emotions were so strong that it almost drove him to utter madness. He longed for just one bite of her insatiable forbidden fruit. Just one bite would make for an irritable delicacy to his hungry drooling lips.

He ripped off her dress and grabbed her bouncing tits. Laura was terrified by his ruthless actions! She wanted to scream but was overwhelmed with shivering fear. He starred at her with an uncontrollable lust and desire. He pulled her close to his chest and whispered in her ear,

"You are mine! I must have you now!" He became more enraged with passion as he watched her. He suddenly unleashed a powerful seduction of heated passion upon her naked body.

Like a huge magnet, the two lovers clashed together as closely knitted as a glove to hand. The juicy nectars flowed fast and potent, until a new life was conceived. Every night for two months they met under the cloak of darkness and made hot blazing love. Thomas became devoted to Laura and wanted to spend every moment in her presence.

Laura grew a powerful fear when she felt her body changing. Her appetite increased. She was always hungry. She thought to herself, "I can't be having the Master's baby! What will happen to me and this child? God please have Mercy on my soul! As strange as Mrs. Revelle been acting, if she finds out of this abomination, she just might have me and the baby killed!"

Frantically, she confided to Candid, the butler, about her God awful predicament. She sworn him to secrecy. He promised to help her. Instead, he ran back to Master Thomas and told him about Laura' pregnancy.

Thomas laughed at the thought of his nigga slave bitch having his baby. His laughter was silenced by the sweet memories of all the long nights of intimate pleasures he shared with her. She had stole his heart and took his breath away. Sparks shot all over his body. Leaving him dripping wet with lustful desires. He decided to visit Laura and relieve her concerns about her unfortunate condition.

Thomas spoke to her calmly, yet he was firm with his words. He said, "So you're going to have a picky ninny huh? Rest your mind Laura. I am not going to hurt you or that baby you're carrying in your belly. Just promise me one thing. Promise me that you will never tell anyone that I am the baby's father! If you ever let those words fly outta your mouth, I will kill you and that brat! Candid will take care of you until you come to full term and push that baby out into this world. You know of course, you'll have to give the baby to me the second it is born. I'll provide a roof over it's head, put food in it's stomach, and make sure it gets a good education. This child will not be a slave. The Mrs and I will care for it like it's our own child. Don't be crying and begging to keep the baby once it's born. If I have to warn you again, you better pray that I'll be in a good mood and have mercy on you! Consider yourself lucky! If I were like the rest of these fine southern gentlemen, I would kill you now and wash my hands of this whole mess!"

Too afraid to speak, Laura shook her head in agreement to his hellish demands. However, each day she carried her baby inside her womb, it grew closer to her heart. She did not want to give her baby away to Master and his wife. She thought of running away, but if the bounty hunters caught her, they would kill her and her unborn baby. She spent many sleepless nights worrying. She prayed that he would have a change of heart and allow her to keep their baby.

Thomas really loved Laura, but he was afraid that if his family found out about her baby before it was born, that they would have Laura strung up from a tree! His wife was low sick and bedridden after having the third miscarriage. The poor woman almost lost her mind when the Doctor told her that the baby was stillborn. For Laura's safety, Master Thomas moved her to a private cabin on the estate.

Laura was so lonely living in the cabin all by herself. Candid was the only visitor she had when he brought her weekly food supplies.

Finally the big day arrived! Laura was going to have her baby. Candid ran to the big house to fetch Master Thomas, but he was out of town on business. He said to Laura, "Don't you fret none girl! I am right here with you! Master Thomas not here so it's just me and you! I will do all I can to help you. Your baby is ready to come out and see the world no matter how cruel it may be. This innocent child can not pay for its father's no good deeds. This baby is flesh of your flesh and blood of your blood. So love it with all your heart!

Laura hollered, "Candid! Please help me! The baby is coming! I'm hurting so bad! My guts are tearing apart! Oh my God! Lord please take the pain away now!" She was soaked with sweat. Candid was in shock. He yelled, "Oh Lord have Mercy on me and this girl! Tell me what to do Jesus! Show me how to help Laura have this baby! I am your servant Lord! Teach me and guide me through this journey! Push Laura push until you can't push no more! Late into the night, Laura gave birth to a son she named him Samuel. His strong cries filled the air with the sound of new life. Master Thomas told Candid to take Laura and little Samuel to his cabin in the woods. There she rested and nursed her new born baby for a week. Master Thomas came to visit Laura and his son.

With a cruel and ruthless heart, he took Samuel right out of her arms! He looked her into her eyes and said, "Listen here you nigga wench! I can't keep you here any longer. My wife is wondering why I spend so much time here at the cabin ". I'm sending you to the fields! You'll be alright! Find yourself one of my boys to keep you company.

Laura was distraught. She begged her Master not to take her baby. She pleaded, "But Thomas, what about my baby? He be my only kin folk. He is my flesh and my blood, and your flesh and your blood. He needs the milk from my breast to live!" Master Thomas was furious he yelled, "Listen here you nigga bitch! I own you just like I own the horses and the cows on this here plantation. If you want this boy to live, you will do what I say! Else I will slit his throat from ear to ear, and slaughter him just like I butcher my hogs in the winter! Don't give me any trouble about this boy! I will take him home to my wife and we will raise him as our own son! At that moment, he took Samuel and left.

Laura was left heartbroken and she cried all the way back to her cabin on the estate. The next day she went to work in the fields. Not a day went by without her thinking about her baby Samuel. Laura regressed to sorrowful and tearful moods. She would call out for Samuel in her sleep. When Master Thomas found out that Laura was calling out for her child, he poured her to his cabin in the woods. In a vengeful rage, he swung his sharp blade and cut off Laura's arm!

Laura would not die! She drugged herself back to the slave quarters and received help from the other slave women. In time she healed and eventually returned to work in the fields. It was in those fields that she met a big strapping buck named Garfield. The pair married and lived happily for a while.

CHAPTER 3

TOM REVELLE'S SON SAMUEL

E ven though Master Thomas said he and his wife would raise little Samuel, he lied! Thomas and his faithful servant Candid raised Samuel in confidential seclusion until he reached the age of seven. At that time he was presented as Master Thomas' nephew.

For his education, teachers were hired under the strictest, private, and most confidential regulations. They were paid a handsome salary for their loyalty and discretion. They agreed not to divulge any knowledge of their pupils' identity or his location.

Candid grew to love little Samuel as his own. When Master Thomas was away on business, Candid allowed lil Samuel to play with the other children that lived in the slave quarters. On a pretty hot summer's day, Samuel played hide and seek with the other kids; running up and down the blooming buds of stinging cotton.

However, the slave parents of the other kids were afraid and reluctant for Samuel to play with their off spring. They worried that he might have gotten hurt, fell, or caught a bloody nose from wrestling. So a few of the parents went to see Candid at his private quarters with lavish furnishings and good food.

Candid knew instantly why they had come knocking at his door. He led them straight to the kitchen. They had not seen such delicious fruits, vegetables, and meat entrees spread on a slave's table before. All they ever had was spoiled left overs that were no longer suitable for the master's table.

Candid said assuredly, "Do not worry. Your children are safe. No harm will come to them. Do not concern yourselves with who his paw be! That is none of your dam business. Keep your mouths shut, and speak to no one else about this matter! Come join me for supper. You are always welcome at my table. I will fix all of you some mighty tasty baskets to take back home and share with your families."

Over the years, Samuel grew to be a fine intelligent handsome man just like his father. Knowledge of Samuel's birth mother being a black slave leaked to unfriendly sources. Mainly relatives who wanted to inherit the entire Revelle fortune. Master Thomas had recently passed away and could no longer protect Samuel from the onslaught of greedy and diabolical maneuvers from his cousins to steal the family estate.

Samuel moved out from the Revelle home in fear for his life and settled in a black neighborhood. There he gained recognition as a powerful clergyman. He was voted the prestigious position of Pastor of the Anna Berry Baptist Church.

He was an eloquent yet boisterous speaker. His sermons sent chills all through the congregation. It raised them up on their feet with standing ovations of praise and worship to the Lord and Savior Jesus Christ. The sisters and deacons were so moved that they joined in a holy dance on the church floor. Chanting Jesus Jesus until they fell into the spirit of worship and spoke in the heavenly language of tongues and were filled with the power of the Holy Ghost.

It was one early Monday morning. Samuel was fixing his lunch before heading out to join the other workers in the bean fields. He was unexpectedly interrupted by a knock at the door. He wondered who could be visiting him at 7am in the morning. As he opened the door, he saw a tall white gentleman dressed in an expensive black tailor maid suit and carrying a large black brief case. Nervously Samuel said, "That's a mighty fine suit you're wearing Sir. May I ask why are you visiting me this morning?" The tall handsome man replied, "I am here on behalf of my anonymous client to deliver a transfer of ownership of land and property to one Samuel Ridley. May I step inside your humble abode to complete this important matter of business?" Samuel replied, "Why yes please come in Sir."

The distinguished gentlemen came inside and seated himself on the couch. He opened his brief case on the coffee table. He presented Samuel with the documents of deeds of ownership for fifty acres of land, a house, and blacksmith shop. He asked Samuel for his signature to complete the transfer of ownership. As soon as the signatures were received, he closed his brief case and left as quickly as he had first arrived.

Samuel was so happy that he jumped high and danced in circles while celebrating his good fortune.

31 LAURA MARIAH, SON SAMUEL AND ALBERTA Thomas and his faithful servant Candy raised Samuel in confidential seclusion until he reached the age of seven. He was presented at that interval as Thomas's nephew. Samuel grew to be a fine, intelligent and handsome man just like his father!!!

SEPTEMBER 1914-1920

Knowledge of Samuel's birth mother being a black slave leaked to unfriendly sources, mainly relatives who wanted to inherit the entire Revelle fortune. His father had recently passed away and could no longer protect him from the onslaught of greedy and diabolical maneuvers of his cousins to steal the family estate.

Samuel moved out from the Revelle home in shame and despair at the extremities of ruthlessness that threatened his life and settled in a black neighborhood where he gained recognition as a powerful clergyman. He was voted the prestigious position of pastor of the Anna Berry Baptist Church.

He was an eloquent yet boisterous speaker! His sermons sent chills although the congregation while raising them up on their feet with standing ovations of praise and worship to the Lord and savior Jesus Christ! The sisters and decons were so moved that they joined in a holy dance on the church floor! Chanting Jesus, Jesus until they fell into the spirit of worship and spoke in the heavenly language of tongues and were filled with the power of the Holy Ghost!!

Samuel poured out his soul, giving all the glory and honor to God as he welcomed members old and new to partake in the procession of communion. The entire church congregation start singing Drinking of The wine, The Holy Wine, in ceremony crackers are broken and placed on a tray to represent the body of Jesus, and wine poured in tiny glasses to represent the blood of Jesus, then the bread and wine is passed around to every member to join in remembrance of God. Then, everyone is invited to the Wonderful Day Of Home Coming! On this day, relatives and friends from all surrounding counties sit down to enjoy -----

CHAPTER 4

SAMUEL MEETS ALBERTA

Alberta was of Cherokee and Black Foot Indian descent. She was given to a local white family to pay off a huge debt owed by her father, Daniel Clerk, at the age of seven. She was to be a maid and helper to old Lady Pittman, who was so large that she could not bend over to tie her own shoes. Her huge frame hindered her from taking care of her family needs. She would pluck Alberta on the head with a licking stick whenever she made an error while cooking or cleaning the big house. It was a tall order for little Alberta to fill. Her chores included house cleaning, cooking, sewing, washing the laundry, and caring for small children too.

After nine years of working for the Pittman family, Alberta found her natural mother Ms. MinevaMineva aka Ms Minnie, as she was fondly called. She told Alberta that her father was a good for nothing bum who left her stranded without any money or a roof over her head. Ms Minnie was so happy to be back with her daughter that she invited her to live with her in her home. Without any hesitation Alberta said yes. Alberta continued to work for the Pittman family to help make ends meet.

Ms Pittman often had Alberta deliver her brothers food and refreshments, while they attended the livestock barn auction sale. The livestock auctioneer were your typical white males only. However, because of who he was, Samuel Ridley was fortunate to land a position as auctioneer also. This left many black residents with raised eyebrows and a bit of jealousy.

On one cool evening while Alberta was making her deliveries to the Pittman brothers, she caught the eyes of Samuel Ridley. Her image lingered in his mind for days. He hoped to see her once again soon.

Ms Minnie noticed Alberta was very lonely and suffered great difficulties adjusting to her new surroundings at home. She talked her into going to the home coming dinner at Anna Berry Baptist Church. She told her that everybody should get a good dose of religion at least once a year. Alberta gave into her mother's wishes and the two of them prepared a box of food for the spectacular event.

She and Alberta cooked a variety of entrees; fried chicken, collard greens, chitterlings, corn bread, butter beans, meat loaf, mashed potatoes, and sweet potato pies. Then the two women loaded the goodies into an old horse and buggy and headed to church. On the way, she and Alberta laughed and sang songs while gazing at the sunlight peering through the trees alongside the road. The members greeted each other with a warm hug as they entered the spiritual celebration. After prayer and a soul stirring sermon, they adjoined to the kitchen for dinner and fellowship.

On this beautiful Sunday evening Samuel and Alberta met once again. This time their eyes met and fire swept all through their bodies. The heat was so hot that the ice in Samuel's glass began popping loudly. As they moved further down towards the desserts, the big sisters of the church noticed Samuel paying too much attention to Alberta, and deliberately bumped into her. Knocking her further down the line Because of church gossip by the jealous sisters, Alberta and Samuel separated for the rest

After service ended, Ms. Minnie and Alberta returned home. Ms Minnie said to Alberta, "Girl how those old gossiping witches were eye balling you. I thought they were going to suffocate you when they squeezed between you and the Pastor. Now Alberta what do you think of our Dear Pastor Sam?"

Alberta replied, "He sure is a powerful man when he preaches!" Uncle Lee, Ms. Minnies' brother, was ease dropping on their conversation from the window. He was a feisty old timer full of mischievous pranks. A busy body. He butted into their conversation and said, "Chile, you aint caught the Reverend yet? What's the matter? Don't let them big sisters scare you away. All you got to do is catch one of those big mouth gals from behind and they will all come tumbling down!" He chuckled. Alberta was not worried about those old bats anyway. She spouted, "I aint chasing no preacher!" Ms. Minnie replied, "Who do you think you fooling? I saw your eyes light up like the moon on a starlit night. The love bug done stung you like a honey bee!"

Uncle Lee told her without hesitation, "Alberta, well now I tell you girl, you better be smart and quick if you want to catch that rooster before some other hen starts cackling and flapping her wings and steal the prize. Sister Betty already pulling pranks outta her bag of tricks. I saw her just smiling and batting those big eyes at Bro Ridley. Then she started shouting and waving her hands like she was caught up in the Holy Spirit speaking in tongues. Then she open her eyes to see who was watching as she faked like she was fainting at the alter." They all laughed.

Ms. Minnie said to Uncle Lee, "Shut up you old fool! You need to mind your own business. Mr. Cupid already shot his arrows into Samuel and Alberta's heart. There is going to be a wedding real soon. I can feel it in my bones. So Uncle Lee, get out your best suit and shine your alligator shoes because you're going to be giving the bride away real soon. Sister Betty may as well cast her eyes on one of those old geezers on the deacon board. She'll be sure to find a sweet daddy over there, but Samuel Ridley has already been spoken for. As Alberta's Momma, I already done dreamed that he will be my son in law. Nobody on this earth can tell me any different. So I'm going too get my old wedding dress ready for my baby girl, and you can give me that blue hanky you carry in your pocket. I will borrow a pearl necklace and buy her a new white lace garter belt. Then I'll stop by Ms. Fannie's Floral Shop and order a lovely bouquet. This will be a grand wedding indeed!"

Filled with so much anticipation, Alberta retired to her tiny bedroom to put together a knock out sexy ensemble that would surely capture the heart of her beloved Samuel Ridley. She spent the entire evening looking through her meager wardrobe. Trying to find the perfect outfit for next Sunday's Worship Service.

Her first choice, she paired up a pretty white blouse with a big collar and puffed sleeves with a long tailored black and white plaid skirt; mustn't forget that black alluring wide brimmed hat and pearl hat pin perched on the side. Her second choice was a two piece elegant white suit with a matching flower hat. The third choice was a pretty bold hot red skirt suit. Which was a hand me down given by Ms Pittman and needed major alterations to yield the perfect fit. Alberta was a highly skilled seamstress. She could make any garment look like it came from a fine department store. Even the patterns drawn and cut out on newspaper.

As night fell on the day, Alberta became enthralled with romantic interludes of Samuel devouring her hungry lips with hot wet vanilla kisses. She longed for the little white house with the picket fence sitting up on a quiet hill. She also envisioned having a house full of beautiful children with her handsome fellow.

The sap was rising. Spring was in full bloom. Fields of wild flowers, honeysuckle, and sweet bubble trees lit up the day with a colorful array of fragrant passion and ecstasy.

If the sisters at the church knew what was on Alberta's mind, they would tan her back side good fashion, wash her mouth out with pot ash soap, make her sit on the front pew, and ask the Good Lord to forgive her for her naughty wicked thoughts.

Sam Ridley had no idea of what was in store for him come the next Sunday Worship. Alberta was bound and determined to win him over with her feminine wilds and sweet potato pie.

Alberta was one of the best cooks in all of Butts County. She was well known for her delicious homemade biscuits and golden brown southern style fried chicken. No one could resist her sweet potato pies.

The following Saturday before the Church Anniversary, she put phase two of her master plan to get her man into action. She gathered all the special ingredients, special spices, onions, vanilla flavoring, and the fattest hen, to prepare a sumptuous meal fit for a king. She was smiling all the while she was busy turning about in the kitchen. She chopped onions, peeled potatoes, made pies, and fried up the bird to put into the family food box for the Church Anniversary dinner.

She picked the perfect outfit, cooked the perfect meal, and was the sexiest hot red momma in her hot red suit. She was going to win her man and walk down that aisle as Mrs. Samuel Ridley. No one not even Sister Betty was going to stand in her way. On that very day, that was exactly what she did.

CHAPTER 5

SAMUEL AND ALBERTA MARRIED
WITH CHILDREN

Every afternoon Alberta sneaked out the back door of her home to listen out for the galloping horses. When she heard that sound, she knew instantly that her lover was on his way. Their loved shined brightly as the pair ventured down the country lane, hand in hand, dreaming of their future together as man and wife. Seldom a word was spoken as they gazed into each others glistening eyes. Samuel wanted lots of children.

They were caught necking by prominent members of the Deacon Board and decided to rush their union to save Samuel's reputation. So wedding plans were made, announcements were sent out, bridesmaids were selected, a best man was chosen, and a maid of honor was chosen. Everything was put into motion for this happy occasion. Alberta had captured Samuel's heart and it bonded to her own heartbeat. There was no room for any foul air to come between them. They were hitched at the hip like siamese twins in all of their thoughts and desires.

Their love was astounding to everyone. Their holy union produced fourteen children. All were delivered by skillful mid wives. Their beautiful family of children consisted of eight girls and six boys. Every spring season a new baby was born. Each child was as lovely as all the pretty flowers that blossomed. Three of their daughters, Evelyn, Ruby, and Marie, had green eyes of fire with thick and curly black hair and a smile that lit up the morning with a fresh cheerful breeze.

On one winter night, while Samuel was away on business, a fierce fire ripped through their family home. Tall flames flew from the chimney. It engulfed the roof with a hot blazing inferno. It was bitter cold that night. Unaware of the cracks in the chimney tower, Alberta had thrown a few extra logs on top of the red hot ashes in the fire place. Waking from a cat nap she smelled smoke in the air and yelled for the children to wake up and take refuge outside of the house. Then she sprang into action. She ordered the kids to form a line from the well to the backside of the house. She ran to the barn and grabbed a ladder and rushed back to the fire area. She climbed up to the top of the roof. Screaming loudly she said, "Boys move quick like lightening and keep the buckets of water coming to me!" Quickly Lidge, one of the older sons, lowered the bucket down into the well and drew up the splashing pail of water while turning the pulley handle forcefully with rapid motion. The other kids passed every pail hastily down the line and back to Alberta. With every dousing on the flames she begged God to spare their home. Alberta yelled, "Help me lord! Please Help me Lord!" God heard her and answered all her prayers.

Samuel worked several odd jobs. This allowed him to work with other black men in town. It was in the fields that he learned the true identity of his birth mother. Samuel was blown away with the astonishing news of his mother being a black woman. How could his Father have been so deceitful to tear him away from his mother. Then send her so far away from the only home and family that she ever known.

He was in total shock to hear about the identity of his birth mother, Laura Mariah. Samuel hurried home to share this wonderful news with Alberta. She was so overwhelmed with great joy and happiness when he told her that his mother was still alive and that he was going to find her and bring her back home to live with the family.

Samuel asked his old friend Stuart if he could drive him down to Sparta, GA to look for his mother. Stuart agreed to take him there, but insisted that Samuel pay for the gas expense for the long trip. Alberta packed a picnic lunch and jar of homemade lemonade, and put them into the back seat of Stuarts' old car. She gave Samuel a long warm hug and wished him much success on his quest to find his dear sainted mother. Tears flowed down her cheeks as she waved good bye as she watched the old plucker drive out of sight.

It was steamy hot inside the vehicle. Stuart rolled down the front windows to catch a breath of fresh air. Somehow they got lost on the out skirts of the town and ended up on a rocky dirt road that led to some rotten old dilapidated shack houses. They saw an elderly woman sitting on her porch and stopped to ask for directions. She looked very malnourished and exhausted. He pretty white hair stood up all over her head. Her eyesight had grown dimmer over the years. She was ninety-eight percent blind. She had a keen sense of hearing and heard Samuel's steps as he nervously walked up the driveway.

Clearing his throat he said, "Hello Ma'am. My friend and I are lost and wondered if you can tell us how to get to Sparta GA? We made a wrong turn and ended up here." The kind old lady motioned for him to sit on her door step. Then she asked, "What entire nation has you out here in all this hot air? You better be careful you don't turn white eyed and have a heat stroke." Samuel began to tell her about his quest to find his dearly beloved mother. He told her, "I was working in the fields down in Butts County when | heard news that my mother was alive and living somewhere down in Sparta. I was taken from her arms when I was first born and never got a chance to tell her how much I love her. She would be about your age I guess. My heart will not rest until I find my dear sweet angel and feel her heartbeat next to mine."

The elderly lady's heartbeat began to beat so strong with great joy and anticipation that this man sitting on her door step could be her long lost son Samuel. She asked, "What is your name?" He replied, "My name is Samuel Ridley." She said, "Well then may I tell you that your journey is over. Your dear mother is here on this porch with you! Yes, Yes Yes I am your mother Laura Mariah!" His eyes wept with tears of joy upon their glorious reunion! The two talked for hours before he carried her home to meet her grandchildren for the very first time.

Laura Mariah held both hands up in the air and looked towards the Heavens and said, "The Lord is good and Merciful! I sat on this porch many times, dreaming about you. Wondering what you would look like and if I had any grand kids. Thank God my prayers have finally been answered. You can't beat God's giving no matter how you try. God has given me the most precious gift of all! He gave me back my heart when he sent you back home to me! Thank you Jesus!"

Laura Mariah knew her time on this earth was coming to its final chapter of life. With every sunrise, her steps became slower. She devoted the rest of her days to loving and caring for her grandchildren. Having an inward discerning spirit, she knew each child by listening their voices. She spent hours sitting near the window listening to the kids play all day.

Young Lidge was a sprankster who loved to play jokes on his little sister Marie. Marie was a tomboy, who loved to follow behind her brothers and their little friends. Lidge spotted Marie hiding behind a tree and nudged his pal in the arm and whispered, "Here she comes again. That's all right we are going to fix her little wagon real good." They had just finished taking a shit in the woods. Quickly they covered the piles of shit with dirt, and added three extra piles of dirt beside them. They ran away laughing and hid in the nearby bushes. When Marie reached the piles, she began squeezing them between her fingers. One by one she worked up each pile until she worked up a pile with shit inside of it. Lidge and his pals fell on the ground laughing real hard. Marie had fell hook, line, and sinker to this nasty smelly prank.

Little Marie ran back to the house where her big sister Tassie was standing on the porch. Marie asked her for a drink of water. When she reached for the glass, Tassie noticed her dirty hands. The rising stench infiltrated her nostrils that made her cough and gag. Tassie yelled, "Uh huh! You been following those boys again! They got you real good this time!" Marie felt sad and began to cry. She said, "I saw Lidge and his friends making mud pies, and I wanted to play with the mud pies too. Now they laughing at me cause my hands stink like poop!"

Tassie poured some water into the basin from the water bucket and gave Marie some of Alberta's homemade soap. She told her to wash her hands real good. Not wanting little Marie to see her laughing, Tassie turned her head towards Laura Mariah's view in the window and they both chuckled and grinned.

During her later years, Laura Mariah's mind greatly deteriorated. It left her in a state of confusion. She would forget present day life and journey into an excursion of days that were once in her past. Some days she would stumble over times where she wailed in pain and agony when old wounds were made new. Bitter scars cut deep into her flesh. Ripping her heart into pieces. As she struggled to survive those awful memories. From the darkness of night to the light of day, she would sing praises up to the Lord. She knew she hadn't much more time to live in her old tired body.

Sometimes Laura Mariah would open her keepsake box and remove an old wooden baby rattle. She would clinch it tightly to her chest and sing sweet tunes of motherly love to an imaginary baby. This rattle was all she had to comfort her during the time that Samuel was taken away from her.

She was blinded from cooking over hot stoves and working out in the fields under the scorching sun. Even though she could not see, she could hear a pin drop at any moment. The children's laughter brought joy into her dark world. Little Marie was her favorite. She was brave and curious and wanted to know everything about life. She often asked why this or why that. Sometimes questions as simple as why does a butterfly have pretty colored wings, or why a chicken had wings but could not fly? Laura Mariah chuckled every time little Marie opened her mouth and asked her no non-sense questions.

One evening Little Marie boldly asked, "Grandma why are you blind? What happened to your arm? Why is my dad white and you are black? Is my Grandfather white too?" These questions put fear in her Grandmother's heart. She was afraid that if she told Lil Marie about her white relatives, she might run away and try to find them. She quickly changed the conversation by telling Lil Marie that she could play with her homemade sock dolls at the foot of her bed. They started playing puppet games and talked about circus animals. She also shared a piece of peppermint candy with Lil Marie. She hoped this would calm her curiosity about the white folk on the other side of the hill.

Her Grandmother calmly said, "Child you sure are nosey. All that matters in life is that you are loved, needed, and wanted. Your mother and father love all you children and would do anything to keep you safe." Lil Marie still had questions. She replied, "Well, I don't know if I am black or white. The other kids make fun of me and call me names. They say I am half and half and call me high yell and then they pull my hair. Grandma replied, "Hush child! Don't let your paw hear you asking me those questions. Don't pay those mean children any mind. They will get what's coming to them soon enough. God don't like ugly. We live in a town where it's a crime if black and white mix. Maybe one day when people change their hateful ways, you can visit your other relatives.

Each morning before doing chores little Marie would take care of her Grandma Laura. She poured fresh rain water into a basin on the dresser that sat in the corner of Laura Mariah's bedroom. She carefully dip a hand towel in the water with soap and gently washed her Grandmother's face. She would gather clean clothes from the chest and lay them out on the foot of her Grandmothers' bed. After getting her bathed and dressed she would sit in her favorite rocking chair as little Marie combed and brushed her long hair. She would sometimes sit in her Grandmother's lap and sneak a pinch of her honey bee snuff. They all would be chewing and spitting out that juice; while laughing and talking about old times. Laura Mariah loved sharing her guarded thoughts with all of her grandchildren.

Seeds of great love and sacrifice were sewn in the gritty soil of life in the cold and sometimes heartless bitter south. Springtime harvest also known as Good Friday. This is the day to gather all the seeds from last year's crops of wheat, corn, peas, butter beans, sweet potato and white potato plants and sew them in the dark rich earth. Samuel hitched up the old mule to the plow and started tilting the soil until it formed patterns of perfect rows.

Everyone in the house rolled up their sleeves, put on their straw hats, and went to work. Lil Marie and all her brothers and sisters worked very hard out in the fields until their little fingers wore sore to the bone. Their clothes would be drenched in stinging sweat. The cows had to be tended, logs had to be cut, eggs gathered, pigs fed, and weeds chopped away from the collard greens and butter bean fields.

Early in the morning gusty winds blew fragrant scents of honeysuckle bouquets through the opened windows of the family home, urging the kids to sneak outside to run and play amongst the bunches of butter cups in the tall grass of the opened fields.

Alberta was a caring and loving mother. She wanted her family to look their best at all times. Tuesday morning was laundry day. On this day she filled the wash tub with fresh rain water and placed a rubbing board inside to scrub the garments squeaky clean. After washing and rinsing each garment, she would secure each piece with wooden pins on clothes lines that stretched north, east, south, and west. Leaving them to dry from the steaming hot sun and the breezy winds.

Wednesday was ironing day. Alberta stripped the clothes from the lines and carried them inside to the back room and tossed them onto an old folding table. She quickly retrieved some split logs from the back porch and chugged them inside the left compartment of her wood burning stove. She placed her smoothing iron on the top of the stove. She stood on her feet for hours ironing each piece until they were silky smooth and wrinkle free. Afterwards, she place each item on the wire hangers and hung them neatly in the closets. After the laundry was done she hurried back into the kitchen to cook a hearty meal for her husband Samuel and all their hungry children, as well as Grandma Laura.

Laura Mariah was a tired broken old woman, but her strength and courage would beem through her heart. She wore thick brown rim glasses on her sunken face, and always wore a long sweeping skirt that kept her bones warm in the cold night air. Hard living had ravished her frail body but not her spirit. She had outlived her cruel evil master and many other enemy's voices had been silenced as well.

Several years had passed. On this particular morning Alberta was taking her usual walk down the country dirt road. She always admired the splendor of mother nature's beauty. She came upon a lovely bed of nestled pink roses nestled among the fallen leaves. She wondered what kind of fertilizer would grant such a miraculous rebirth season after season. She thought that underneath the dirt and roots may very well have been the heart and soul of a lost spirit trying to find his way back home.

In those days, greedy relatives murdered their own family members; then accused innocent black men and women for their hideous slayings. Such was the story of Evan, Alberta's long lost nephew. He was accused of splitting old man Hampton's head wide open with an axe. He was found guilty of murder and hanged from a tall oak tree. His hanging was an example of power and put fear in the hearts of all black residents in Jason County. Evan was laid to rest in the backyard of his mother's home near the pecan tree where he had once gathered nuts to sell at the market place. Five years later he was cleared of the crime by a death bed confession of the guilty party!

Evelyn and Marie one to the fields to pick some butter beans for supper. It was Charles turn but he was too busy listening to the news their father brought from town. Charles came running down the rows of beans yelling, "Did you hear the news about cousin Chester?"

Cousin Chester was a farm hand for the Hodges family. They had a lovely daughter named Catherine. Catherine and Chester were secret lovers. Her father became suspicious when he caught them holding hands in the barn. He conspired a way to catch them in their very act. He told Catherine that the family was going on a business trip out of town. Her father packed suitcases and placed them on the rumble seat of his automobile and gathered everyone except Catherine. She was instructed to remain home to greet some important salesman the next day. Longing to feel the fire of Chester's love, she happily agreed to stay home. Chester knew he was committing the sin of all sins, at least in the white man's eyes. She couldn't wait to feel his big black muscular body laying next to her pale white skin. As night came, she invited Chester to her room. There they greeted each other with an embrace an soft kiss. They passionately undressed each other to the bare skin. They fell in lust and desire onto the bed. The love making that they shared was undeniable. The way he held body made her feel as if she were in paradise. She love the very ground he walked on.

Mr. Hodges made some excuse that he had left some papers and returned home. Tipping up the stairs of their home, he could her their soothing moans of ecstasy. He pushed Catherine's bedroom door opened and saw the two of the naked in bed. Chester jumped up, snatched his clothes, and ran away. Catherine was too afraid to tell her father of her love for Chester. She screamed to the top of her lungs "RAPE!" Mr Hodges knew his daughter was lying, but he went along with her tale because of his pride.

Forming a mob, they tracked Chester down in the woods. The mob beat Chester with a whip until his skin burst wide open. Then one of the mobster cut off his penis with a boa knife and stuck it inside of his mouth. After which they riddled him with hundreds of bullets from their rifles and handguns. They threw his mutilated body in Willow's Pond. His body was seen floating down stream behind his old hat.

The angry south had no moral conscience and continued its murderous rampage on black people. The mighty rivers ran cold with innocent blood flowing down stream. Unmarked and watered graves help many skeletal remains. Interracial dating was a sure fire death sentence for anyone who crossed that line.

Chester's murder was one of the many heinous crimes committed against young black men in Butts Country. At one point it was not safe for a black man to even look or speak to a white woman. Samuel's boys were sick and afraid of all the hate and prejudice that infiltrated their world. Their means of escape was to march to the call of Uncle Sam. Each young man stepped bravely up to the plate of honor to defend their country. They joined the army leaving all the chores for the girls and their parents.

The work was hard and strenuous and left no time for fun or folly. Samuel worked from sun up to sun down to keep food on the table for his remaining family. Sugar was rationed proportionately as was meat and flour. Some vegetables and poultry were traded at the local merchant store. Coffee, corn meal, and a special treat of peppermint sticks, for the younger girls, were some of the item batered.

Alberta's prayers for the safe return of her boys were uttered throughout the long restless nights. She would bow down on her knees with her face turned towards the Heavens asking the Lord to watch over her boys and to keep them safe from the enemies bullets.

Unable to read or write, she would get Marie to write her brothers every week. Marie listened very carefully as Alberta dictated words of love and great concerns for her brave soldier boys. The letters were always aligned with a message for them to always pray for their safe journey back home.

Lewis, Lidge, and Charles were pleased to receive news from home. The words drew pictures from their memories of the good times when they played up and down the muddy roads as young boys. They played with frogs and lizards, and played nasty little pranks on their sisters. Charles often reminisced about the delicious aroma of his mother's apple pies. He would dash to the kitchen to sneak a taste of the stewed apples brewing in the pot. All those treasured memories help them to survive the cold and bitter nights. Most nights were lit up with blazing rapid artillery fire. They would crawl on their bellies; drinking their tears while praying for the morning sun to come and warm their tired cold shivering bodies.

As young boys, they had learned how to run fast like jack rabbits. They could hide and blend in with Mother Nature's garden of trees, vines, and wild flowers, and could not be seen in plain sight. They were very well skilled in survival techniques, bate and switch, back tracking, and careful aiming to hit the designated targets. Many days they had gone to the woods with their father's old shot gun and brought back wild ducks, rabbits, and possums for a hearty and tasteful supper.

Charles often joked in his letters about being a fish out of water during his enlisted duties overseas... The waves toppled over the ship that housed the scarred dampened men. Some of them complained of sea sickness. A soldier was swept off the side of the boat just as a wave smashed against the walls of the iron vessel.

Paris, the city of love. There were many ancient relics of the past that withstood the test of time. The city of Marseille on the shore of Mediterranean Sea. On the "Clock Street," a famous medieval landmark in Rowen, the city where Joan of Arc was burned as a stake. A colossal time piece that help the secrets of yesterday. The mountains and hills were covered with flowers. The fragrant petals were picked and used to make the famous perfumes of France. The building cluttered together like cardboard boxes and the fishing boats lined the martigues, Housing quarters dated from the fifteen century.

After much of a difficult journey across the seas. Charles along with his platoon docked on the watery shores of France.

The girls were as pretty as orquets. They were fast, fiery, and craved the GI from America. Charlse chance to meet one of these rare visions of loveliness. Her name was Helena. A cold raven haired beauty with a tongue as sharp as a snake and a body that set your soul to flames. She knew what she wanted and had the ammunition to get it!

Charles fell helplessly in love with Helena. He wanted to marry her. Helena was a black widow spider, she collected hearts in her web and devoured them with the fire of her venomous bite. She could not belong to one man. Charles was a victim of his heart. He received a hilarious laughter to his proposal of marriage.

MAY 1940

France was disarmed. Suddenly, a dark cloud hovered over the fun city. The sirens roared, a black-out!! The Germans were attacking from the air. Building exploded, panic was rampant! Casualties were rapid in number! The civilians and soldiers were evacuated. French villages were destroyed by the onrushing German offensive of May. France was disarmed, stripped of its natural beauty. All trades, shipping and communications were placed under direct axis control. The French people were required to pay the costs of the occupation and to supply the man power and labor necessary for the repair of damaged railroads, docks, and other facilities needed by the Germans. The conquest of France enabled the Germans to complete a huge network of air and submarine bases extending along the western coasts of the European Mainland from the artic oceans to the pyneness mountains.

Helena found a haven in the quarters of the German officers. She was moralless, the mistress of all the men of the German infantry., often adorning herself in the uniform of her lover and playing a vicious officer taking advantage of deathly officer. Her lovers lavished expensive gifts to her only, to watch her dance in a childly manner displaying her pleasure.

GOOD TIME CHARLIE GOT THE BLUES
MARCH 3, 1942

Finally, the B1 Bomber airplanes arrived to save the day! The Germans were counter attacked by the fearless warriors in the sky! The black clouds lit up with thunderous bolts of artillery fired by the freedom knight pilots! With careful precision and marksmanship, they flew over the designated target, dropping those massive B-17 bombs that annihilated every target area!

On the ground front, a group of special infantry unit of American soldiers fought a courageous battle to secure the necessary strong hold to defeat the Nazi regime! Uncle Charles said that he was in one of those brave battalions sprinkled on the ground to do battle against blood the thirsty nemesis!

As he labored in the heated battle of warfare, his heart, mind, body and soul still belonged to his beloved Helena!! In the back of his mind he harbored thoughts of finding her and bringing her back home to live with him and his family!

Machine guns fire of riveting bullets flew in the air like popcorn! Streets were covered with blood and bodies falling left and right! The scent of death was overwhelming to any conscious reasoning! That war was pure hell for Charles and his fellow soldiers! The pilots kept on hurling those bombs and lightening up the skies like a Fourth of July celebration!!

Upon reaching the Gutted out German Headquarters, Charles saw Helena for the last time! There she was nearly dead, laid on the floor next to the enemy! Charles rushed to her side as she uttered her last words!

HELENA------------ My dearest Love, I tried to wait for you, but I feel the life slipping from my battered soul! These eyes and these lips will always love you my darling! There is nothing to forgive! For Love will last forever! Tears fell down his gritty face as he knelt down beside her and held her in his arms and wiped away the blood trickling down her cheeks, then filled her face with oodles of soft gentle kisses!

Two months later, Charles was transferred to a medical facility. While in route to his destination, the ship was attacked, causing Charles to be severely injured! He was returned to the States where he drowned the rest of his life in a bottle! He could not forget the gentleness of Helena's touch or her big beautiful eyes or the way her face lit up when she shared her bright sunny smile!! Each day he dimed her memory with one drink after another! Yes, Uncle Charley became the town drunk! Whether he was thumping his fingers between his knuckles, blowing air music into a jelly jar, or playing hambone with hand slaps across his knees and thighs, he danced to the tune of his own drummer as a clown to hide his broken heart!!!

My mother's brother, Uncle Charlie came to live with us in the early spring of March. He had found out that his previous land lord, cousin Touger had been stealing his money and overcharging him for watered down moon shine! After he paid his rent and liquor bill he was out of cash for the rest of the month! He was a funny character who always liked to tell a joke and poke fun at anything and anybody! He could make up a song about an ant hill jack the rabbit or the monkeys in the jungle! Each morning as the sun rose on a brand new day, you could find him shuffling along in a drunken stupor! He performed the muddle speech and goofy song and dance routine for ten years as an alcoholic! His nudging jesters and idle chatter amused me so much until, one day when I looked into his face and saw his sad eyes staring back at me!

Old Troop as he was called was a World War two Veteran, decorated with metals for acts of bravery, great sacrifice and heroism during a time of heated combat! How tragic that the brave strength and courage that he had exhibited on the bloody grounds of war had been defeated by his own hand each time he sipped the last drop of booze from the bottom of the bottle!!

Curious to know, I asked him why he drunk so much liquor? His reply was that he was a lonely old man forgotten by time! He carried a faded out picture of a beautiful lady in his wallet at all times! I saw him shedding many tears over this picture while shaking his head from side to side and raising his glass in toast to his beloved Helena!

Everyday he and his drinking buddies down in Buttermilk Bottom use to scrape their pennies and nickels together to buy that awful moon shine! The gathering of the elite bums and liars refused to believe in a brighter future, and preferred to soothe the constant pains of failure by sedating their brains and lungs with so much liquor that they couldn't remember the time of day, where they lived or even their own names! The queen of the rowdy crew, Miss Betty Joe, would serve up a spirited tap dance and hilarious comedy skit just by being her natural self! Wearing her crooked wig and long skirt, she would sweep the yard clean as she swung her hands in the air and kicked up the dust with her magic shoes! She always said that all she ever needed was a strong man with a strong back to jump on top of her and ride until kingdom come!! Not having sex with a man for years, she would give him a powerful thrill that he would never forget!!

There was no sugar to be poured on Miss Betty Joe's pitiful pleas for sexual gratification!! Charlie and his scandalous cohorts were too much in love with their unholy communion ritual of drinking, than to be chasing women's skirts! ALL-Of-his buddies had since passed away. Some days poor Charlie would lie in bed, his stomach contracting in aching convulsions, promising to never touch another drop if the Lord would let let him see tomorrow. This was his repintive prayer to God. Early next morning he would stepp lively as a proud soldier to the nearest liquor house where he filled his mouth to over whelming capacity, guzzling spirits like a man dying of thirst.

During the night he became abusive and violent when his supply had depleted, often pacing up and down the hallway swearing that someone stole his booze. Overcomed with fear, I locked my bedroom door, seeking refuge under the bed while I cried myself to sleep.

Each day I woke early in order to prepare breakfast. In an iron skillet I cooked a hearty meal of bacon and eyys sunny side up, homemade biscuits, hot grits with red-eye gravy, coffee and juice. Charles in a grauling mood pushed food awy snarling insulting remarks remarks before rushing out the door to the nearest pub.

He took ill while while strolling in the noon day sun. Charles was rushed to emergency entrance of the Veteran's Hospital. His condition was diagnosed as acute alcoholism and scerosis of the liver. It was recommended that he should be transferred to admission into the hospital to recieve medication and therapy.

Charles was furious, he threatened to kill everybody if we complied with the doctor's recommendations. Uncle Charles vehemently denied that he was an alcoholic right up to the day he died! He always said that he was in complete control and could stop cold turkey, whenever he wanted, but somehow that day never came!

Looking upon his frail and decaying body, I could see that he was near the brink of death doors! His long wavy locks were the only reminder of his youthful years that had with stood the test of time of his weak and trembling soul!

He received treatment and medication for his illnesses at the Veterans Hospital! However, do to the high intake of alcoholic beverages that he swallowed in a doggish haste for all those years had done irreversible damage to his liver and also left him with colon cancer!

Unable to eat by mouth ore intravenously, he was reduced to mere skin and bones! With his last breath of life on this earth, he pleaded for one last dollar shot of vodka and a cigarette!

Telling a funny joke and humming a down home blues tune, he encouraged me to follow my dreams wherever they would lead me! What ever dream I dreamed, I could achieve it as long as I believed in myself as he also believed in me!!

This man taught me to enjoy life to its fullest potential! To never allow the sun to set on this lovely red rose and turn it into a faded image of yesterday!

No longer a woman drifting in a sea of broken dreams, I reach into the heavens and pick those precious gifts of love, peace and happiness and have my heaven right down here on this earth!!!

CHAPTER 6

THE GIRLS ADVENTURE TO
MR. BUBBA'S JUKE JOINT

One hot summer night, the girls plotted to sneak out their bedroom window and go to Mr. Bubba's Juke Joint. All evening the primped in front of the mirror. They brushed and styled their long thick black tailbone length hair until it was perfect. They puckered and painted their lips a bright cherry red. They dabbed a bit of sweet smelling perfume behind their ears. It was sent to them from their brothers Lewis and Lidge, all the way from Paris, France. They slid on their matching pairs of sheer nylon stockings with seems in the back. Tip toeing around the room, the girls continued to primping and modeling in front of the looking glass the entire evening. They looked so pretty all dolled up in their wide tailed skirts, dresses, and ruffled blouses.

They guys were waiting at Mr. Bubba's Juke Joint. They were very eager to meet and greet these hot fine young babes. One of the gents put a nickel in the piccolo and started bobbing his head to a Louis Jordon tune. Hand in hand, the other fellows grabbed the girls and started swinging and swaying, dipping and flipping, truck dancing and jitter bugging to the blaring sounds coming out of the music box. The song came on about doing the truck dance. Marie broke loose and started trucking and Suzy Q'ing all over the floor. The song lyrics went something like this, "Let me tell you the things to do. It's always something new. When you get tired of trucking too. Stop trucking the Suzy Q!" Marie moved her feet back and forth. Twirling her fingers in the air. She shimmed her body left and right, then stood still and did the freeze.

Those big time spenders planked a dollar on the counter and told Mr. Bubba to keep the pop and peanuts coming. Laughing and admiring the young folks from afar, he made sure he earned every cent out of that dollar bill.

Still in a jovial mood on their way back home, Tassie let loose singing loudly a blues tune called 'How Long, Baby How Long'. Snapping and popping their fingers, Sarah and Marie followed behind giggling and talking about how cute the young dudes were and how much fun they had at Mr. Bubba's place.

Alberta woke up at midnight and went to check on the girls. She discovered that they had snuck out through the bedroom window. Awaking from her sleep, little Evelyn spilled the beans on her sisters, because she was not allowed to go with them.

Alberta was standing outside on the front porch when she heard the girls walking up the road still singing and laughing. She hastily ran to the girls bedroom and hid in the closet. Allowing them to crawl back through the window and nestle between the covers. Suddenly she jumped from the closet and began whipping their asses with a brush broom switch. She scolded them for their bad behavior. She yelled, "I heard ya'll coming up the street singing that mess! Tassie I told you about singing them blues. I better not ever hear you singing that evil Jezebel mess again. Come Sunday morning all ya'll going to church. And you better be sitting on the front pew! Tassie you better be up in the choir singing strong and loud to your maker . . . my sweet Jesus! Do you hear me!" Tassie was trembling in fear and could not answer. Alberta repeated herself again in a more angry tone. "I said do you hear me gurl!" Tassie, in a panic state, answered, "Yes Ma'am I hear you loud and clear."

Mommee Alberta's first child little Lucille died from a childhood disease! She was only four years old! Her passing was a devastating loss to Samuel and Alberta! However, the unbreakable bond of love and devotion they shared yielded a lovely bouquet of pretty babies! Their names were as follows; Ruby, Tassie, Julia, Laura, Marie, and Evelyn! They were fondly known as the Ridley girls! Each had their very own unique personalities!

She also welcomed a host of strong boys to the Ridley clan as well! Their names were; Bloomer, Sammie Lee, Obie, Liezghe, and baby

Lewis! They were remembered as the brave Ridley Soldiers for their military service in the Army military!

Aunt Evelyn was the pin up girl of her day! She had a sexy walk with a sexy talk that made the men all pause when she walked by! She was a beautiful, vivacious young lady, full of excitement and adventure, she even took a picture with Roy Rogers and his horse Trigger at the State Fair! She had a scandalous affair with a Baptist minister, Elliot Lockford! Their secret rendezvous was held in the room of the pastor's study at Church!

Aunt Ruby Lin was the intellectual beauty and brains type of girl! With only a high school grade education, she became a teacher at the local high school in Butts Co. She met and fell madly in love with a fellow professor and married into a ready made family! She literally worked herself almost to death everyday taking care of her husband and his seven children! Her husband, Nevelle was mean, cruel and unappreciative of all the great sacrifices she made for him and all his kids! All he wanted was a live in maid, servant and nanny for his brood of unruly brats!!

After ten years of marriage, he ran off with another woman! Leaving Ruby Lin alone to care for all of his kids! She and the kids banded together to survive the awful betrayal of their father! They endured many hardships during those difficult times! Sometimes all they had for supper was a hearty bowl of black eyed peas and corn bread!

After living with the other woman Elvira Mirks, their father became incapacitated, unable to care for himself, he returned to the caring and nurturing arms of Rubin Lin! She was angelically forgiving and opened her loving arms to greet her cheating dog of a husband and welcome him back to the family fold!!

When Nevelle died, Ruby Lin, went to New York to live with Nevelle's daughter that she had raised as her very own child!!!

CHAPTER 7

MARIE'S DREAM OF LEAVING THE FARM

E velyn, Tassie, and Marie went to the Sweetheart Ball on Valentines' Day at their High School. As they walked up to the entrance all was silent. Suddenly music blasted out of a nearby window. Curious, Tassie opened the door. Out on the floor hollering and kicking up a storm, was a young black couple. They were jitterbugging to the swing of the melody coming from the jukebox. They were shaking in the valley like a leaf on a tree. They were really dancing to the beat. It was Walter also known as Big Daddio. He and Big Henrietta were cutting a rug on the dance floor. Cheers rang out from the bar, "Go Daddio! Swing it Big Mamma!"

Walter was a handsome soldier boy fresh from the Navy. He was the best looking man in town. All the girls were after him. He was an imitation of Cab Calloway. Big Daddio was a very attractive man dressed in his three piece zoot suit with gold chains hanging at the waist, a smart brim hat crowning his head, and Cadillac shoes dancing on his feet. Marie was hypnotized by his sexy dance moves. It was love at first. She found him irresistible. Evelyn clapped her hands to his rhythmic tap. Big Daddio noticed his captive audience. He caught a glimpse of Marie as he looked into the mirror behind the bar. He yelled to her, "Hey Baby! Don't go nowhere! Big Daddio wants to swing with you later!"

Every man in the place had their eyes on the Ridley girls. The other women noticed their men watching the beautiful sisters and became enraged with jealousy. As the tune ended, Big Daddio rushed to Marie's side and pulled her in a very dark corner. He spoke seductively, "Just let me look at you, you cuttie pie. You are the apple of my eye. What's your name baby?" She shyly answered, "I'm Marie". "I've never seen you on this side of town before." „he replied. "I don't get out that much.", she exclaimed. Big Daddio looked into her eyes and said, "Baby, don't be shame. I ain't playing no games. I'm just out of the Navy. I gotta shiny ride outside and you can ride in it anytime. Are you ready to go?" Marie said, "I don't know about that! Please excuse me for a moment. I have to go to the little girls room."

Marie walked across the floor where Evelyn was standing. She motioned for Evelyn to follow her to the bathroom. Marie excitingly asked Evelyn, "Did you see that dude Big Daddio? He pulled me to the corner and was talking strong. Ooo he's so handsome. His eyes look so dreamy. I think he wants to marry me!" They both laughed. Evelyn said, "Now Marie I'm only fifteen years old and I know better than that! Honey that's just a line!". But he's so cute!", Marie said.

Marie didn't care if it was a line or not. For her it was love at first sight. It was getting late and Evelyn began to worry and suggested that they leave immediately. The two of them quickly walked outside to find Tassie talking to Big Daddio. Evelyn said to Marie, "Oh no!! bet she gonna tell him where we live! Come on Marie lets get Tassie and get the hell out of this place!". Marie said goodbye to Big Daddio. A warm emotion stuck in her heart. Saying goodbye ached her throat like a piece of ice. He would be the only an she would ever love.

The girls chuckled and joked as they walked back home through the woods. That night Marie was restless in bed. "Evelyn, are you sleep?", she asked. "How can I sleep with you tossing and turning about!". Marie rattled on, "I wonder if he was serious! I'm so tired of working in these fields everyday! Chopping and hoeing until my hands are full of blisters and corns. I don't want to be a farm girl all my life. I want to be a dancer. Me and Big Daddio can dance our way to the stars. Just like Fred Astaire and Ginger Rogers." Evelyn yawned and said, "Shut up dreaming! You better get ready for tomorrow's chores!"

Morning came with a rainbow in the sky as they chopped in the moist soil until noon. The sun beat heavily on their heads as sweat ran down their cheeks like rain.

Four months had past since Marie last seen Walter aka Big Daddio, the love of her life. Day in and day out, Marie did the same old thing.

Making the same steps int he same tracks, stooping and bending, going up and down the rows of cotton. Picking it so fast that her fingers began to ache and cramp. She worked so hard outside in the hot sun until her pale skin was cooked to a caramel brown color.

Even though Marie worked along beside the other pickers in the fields, she experienced hostilities and prejudices from the other back women. Panda was a mean and evil woman with a mouth full of hateful words. If looks could kill, her big angry bulging eyes would have instantly blown Marie's body into bits and pieces.

Whenever the water line was formed, Panda would push Marie out of line and take her place. Daily she would laugh, joke, and tease at Marie. All the other workers were afraid to challenge Panda's bullish controlling nature. She was a bitch and didn't give a damn who knew it. One evening she forced one of the other women to join her in a devious and treacherous plot. She wanted to make sure that Marie would not take another breath of life on top side of the earth before the sun set that evening!"

Panda said to her accomplice, "Listen here bitch! You better do what I tell you to do! I am going to lure Marie away from the water line come break time. When she and I start to fight, I am going to push her down onto the bale of cotton. Then you sneak up and lite the cotton with a match and we'll have us a Marie marshmallow pop!" Grabbing the woman by the collar and yanking her face up close to hers she said, "If you tell anybody our plan, I will spit in your face and stomp you into the ground like a bug!"

The field boss rang the bell to signal that it was time for a water break. Marie working feverishly at her job did not hear the bell or pay any attention to the bale of cotton smoldering nearby. Checking to see if all the other field hands were on water break, Panda put her deadly plan into operation! She grinned and cheered as she came closer to pushing Marie into the burning flames of cotton!

Marie's sister Evelyn noticed Panda sneaking up on her and wondered why they were still in the fields. Just as Panda was about to push Marie into the fire, Evelyn leaped over the rows of cotton and pushed her sister to safety. In panic they watched as the flames soar up into the skies!

Lying through her teeth, Panda yelled, "Boss! Boss! These two no account girls set this bale of cotton on fire and tried to burn me to death!" The field boss was suspicious and didn't believe a word she said. He asked, "Are you up to one of your tricks again?" "No Sir, I'm just trying to help save the field from being destroyed!", she conniving. The fields boss yelled to her, "Something's just not right here! I think you are lying to me! Get back to work! | am the boss out here and don't you forget it!"

Panda let out a wicked laugh and strutted out the fields. Marie knew her life was in danger. She must find a way to save herself from Panda's insane jealousy. Marie's expectation of the ordeal with Panda was intense. She knew it wasn't halfway over. She always looked over both shoulders because she knew that another confrontation with Panda would happen soon.

Marie was wondering if Walter was serious about taking her away from the farm. She prayed to God for this moment to come true and for her protection. She thought, "I wanna live! Protect me from that evil and deadly witch, Panda! Send Walter back to me! Please Lord!"

Exhausted from the work in the field, Marie quickly fell asleep. She began dreaming about Panda. In her nightmare, she heard Panda's wicked laughter. It was dark. She was in the field trying to find her way out when she stumbled over something. It was Panda's head rising up from the ground. Her eyes and mouth were like fire. Marie tried to run but couldn't move. Panda began to spit out fire in the field. Marie screamed so loud that the sound vibrated in her ears, but no-one else heard her desperate cries. She sat up in bed in a wild screaming fit. She was relieved to know that it was only a dream. As she laid in bed starring at the ceiling, she thought about running away from home. She wondered where she would get a few dollars to buy food and a place to stay. Marie shook Evelyn awake and the two of them plotted their escape to a new life in the city. Evelyn was a bit reluctant to leave home, but Marie convinced her to agree with the plan. Marie prayed that Walter would keep his promise and take her with him when he left town.

The next evening the girls were walking back to the house for supper. Marie noticed a long black shiny ford coming up the road. Probably some salesman she thought. She kept hearing someone call her name as she neared the narrow road. It was Walter! Marie yelled to Evelyn, "Ho No it's him!" Evelyn asked, "What are you going to do?" Walter walked up to Marie and said, "Hello there Marie. Listen I don't have much time. I am leaving for Atlanta for an audition as a dancer. Will you come with me? I'll even marry you now! Please say yes!" Marie looked at the long field of cotton and gave a sigh of relief. "Yes! Yes! Yes!" she answered.

They were married at the county courthouse and left for Atlanta that same day. Walter however, was disappointed because he didn't get a chance to audition being that there were so many other black dancers to audition. The agency could not handle them all. Marie and Walter settled in Atlanta. They moved in with Marie's oldest sister Sarah and her husband Leon. Walter became a blue collar worker and Marie became a house wife.

Two hearts met and fell in love. Marie and Walter were united in wedded bliss! The two star crossed lovers were closely knitted together like matching pairs of macrame bed pillows. Outside in the woods of mother nature's scenic beauty, the intoxicating and fragrant flowers of love showered down raindrops of heated passions and ecstasy all over their naked bodies.

Sarah's husband Leon was a slick smooth talking con man. They bought a big rooming house that set high up on a tall hill on Garbalia Street. Walter and Marie lived there for almost a year and a half. Their first born Walter Jr was home delivered by a stately mid-wife named Ms Scott. She told Marie not to worry because she had brought a lot of babies into the world, and that she knew exactly what she was doing. The labor was long and strenuous. Marie let out wailing screams every time the birthing pains riddled through her entire body. She pushed with all her might to bring little Walter into the world. Shortly after midnight, Walter heard his son's voice for the first time when Ms Scott slapped him across his little buttocks. She cleaned him up real good and then called for his father and the rest of the family to come and see that big fine baby boy. He tipped the scale at eight pounds. He had a head full of black curly hair.

Weeks later Walter paid his fair share of the rent and utilities as usual. However, Leon had messed up with the moneyed the gas was cut off. With no heat to keep the new born warm, he became gravely ill with bronchitis pneumonia. Walter cut wood from the fallen limbs and made a fire in the fireplace to keep Marie and the baby warm. He knew he had to find a better and more secure home for his family. So he moved his young family back to Jackson to live with his parents temporarily. Six months later they moved into a four room shack house in Locust Grove. Marie was very excited to finally have their own home.

Locust Grove was a one horse town with businesses located on only one side of the highway. Jobs were next to none, unless you worked in the cotton or butterbean fields. Walter found a job in Dekalb County working with a garbage detail crew.

Love grew stronger every day. Walter and Marie couldn't keep their hands off of each other. Over the years, their once small family grew from one child into a total of eleven children; four girls and seven boys. The kids grew up fast. To make ends meet, Marie and the older kids worked in the fields.

Marie loved her new home even though it did not have running water or indoor plumbing. They enjoyed sitting on their huge front porch nearly every evening. The well stood close to the house. The out house was a distance away to keep those foul odors from stinging their nostrils. Marie had a vegetable garden in the front yard. They raised a lot of baby chicks and had one pig. The boys slopped the hog, while the girls gathered the fresh eggs from the coop. The kids kept the yard swept cleaned with an old fashioned brush broom made from tree branches.

One afternoon, while both parents were away, the Lawrence children decided to prepare their own feast. The oldest sibling Walt Jr, chased the fattest chicken by knocking her out cold with his shoe. Then Mahalie, the next to the oldest, picked off all the feathers and stripped it from it's guts, and threw it into a pot of scalding hot water before cutting her into pieces. She seasoned and battered the sections and fried them up real good in an opened hot skillet. That was some real tasty southern style fried chicken. Well worth the ass whopping they all got later.

During the time of civil unrest, society was immorally unconscious of its murderous misdeeds of human sacrifices, black men hang by their necks from tall oaks! Blood ran cold upon the pillars of blind justice, silencing the tears of grieving mothers who watched in horror the brutal assassinations of their precious loved ones!

Through all the torturous killings, a lonely sailor and a sharecropper's daughter embraced, holding each other so warm and tenderly! From the first moment their eyes met, they were smitten with adoring affection!

While their surviving children still road in the back of the bus, brave African American soldiers that paid the ultimate price for their country, came home in a pine coffin!! Father survived the heated battle on foreign land, only to come home and be slaughtered by the evil henchmen of St Lucifer himself! And Why? Because of greed, lies, and rumors that he was married to a white woman! "Whose to say what we might have become if father had lived and not died?? Still, we are all survivors who take what life dishes out with a tear and a smile and hope for a better tomorrow to ease the pain of yesterday's sorrow!!!!

The bitter south roared with an angry voice of hate, poverty and disease! My father had served his country for four years in the navy, however, upon his return to Georgia, he was denied the Veteran's benefits and respect due him because he was a black man!

Blacks and whites were separated by a railroad track, one side called Dark Town, where the negroes lived in little shanty houses with no bathrooms or inside plumbing. The other side Pep Town, was where the white people lived in larger houses with bay windows, indoor plumbing and electricity. Those separate but equal facilities were not fair balanced at all! My father was hurt and disappointed to find that his home town of Jackson had not changed since stint in the military! His one joy in life was the love that he shared with my mother, Mariah Marie! I was created from the passionate flames that burned within their flesh!!!!!

The only job available to him was that of a garbage collector. Yet, he held his head proudly as he rode outside the back of the dump truck, humping large barrels of trash as his shoulders and hands ached to the bare bones!!

On other occasions they went out into the woods looking for wild berries and plums. Sometimes they would find plum trees loaded with the most big sweet juicy yellow plums. There were under ground springs inside the muddy clay banks. All you had to do was find a stick and poke a hole deep inside the mud to allow the trapped rain water to escape to the surface. The boys would pick blackberries and sell them for fifty cents a pale. Marie could make the best strawberry and blackberry pies. She had learned all her culinary skills from her mother Alberta.

The family pet was a dog named Whitey. He was a smart dog, pure breed German shepherd with white fur and a pink nose. Fearless, he would run ahead of us in the woods making sure the path was safe and free of any harmful reptiles. The dog had a sixth sense and knew when something was not right. Every evening he knew precisely when Walter would be coming home from work. He would run down the road to the rail road tracks and greet his master with a barking solute and playful turn.

Wednesday was washing day for the baby's cloth diapers. Nobody wanted to do that stinky chore. Marie chose the oldest son and daughter to take turns. She had an old wash potshot she poured the water into and heated it by building a fire underneath its belly. As the water got hot, Walt Jr and Mahaile would shake the poop from the diapers by slamming them on the trunk of an old pine tree. Then they threw them into the pot and added some homade lye soap and let them soak before pulling them out with a stick and rinsing them in some cool fresh water.

Friday was payday. The kids looked forward to their father stopping by the package store and buying a couple of barbecue chickens and soda pop. This was the day we celebrated the delicious feast.

CHAPTER 8

THE FAMILY CRISIS

Marie's family was blessed with a bountiful array of children that left her in an urgent dilemma! She often worried about how she was going to feed all of her growing family? Walter was employed by the city of Atlanta sanitation department as a garbage collector Whether it was hot or cold, wet and rainy outside, he got up every morning to go to work He would hold on to the back of the dump truck, hopping off onto the streets to pick up garbage and tossing it up into the back of the trash compact crusher! He did what he had to do in order to provide for his family! With so many mouths to feed, they all endured great struggles to survive!

Growing weary of listening to her children cries for food, Marie hurried to the kitchen, opened the cabinet doors and was so disgusted to find that they were empty to the bare walls! She checked the refrigerator and found a few eggs and slices of fat back! She a 2 pound bag of corn meal on the counter and started to prepare an inventive meal! Placing a skillet on the stove, she allowed it to heat up before placing the slices of fat back inside the hot sizzling grease. This was the recipe she used; 2 cups of water, 3 cups of corn meal, 3 slices of fat back, and 3 eggs. As the corn meal cooked to a creamy consistency like grits, part of the fat back drippings was tossed into the mix to flavor the pot. Marie also fried up some corn bread griddle Cakes and eggs to add to this hardy meal! All the kids gathered around the table with bowls and spoons in hand and ate until their bellies were good and full!

Father use to bring discarded food produce, old loaves of stale bread, cinnamon rolls and half rotten vegetables to feed his hogs! It was our job

45

to feed the stinking animals. I was so hungry that I sneaked a package of cinnamon buns and ran behind the chimney to eagerly devour this sweet and tasty treat. I don't know whether my hunger affected my taste buds, but, that snack was so delicious. Mother heard me munching on the crusty rolls and immediately snatched it from my hand. She said those old buns might make me sick. I didn't want to hear that and begin to cry! That Friday father got paid and mother bought me a whole pack of cinnamon rolls! I took one out for myself and passed the rest on to all my brothers and sisters! We all smacked our lips and licked our fingers while eating those sugary treats. Mother was so happy to see all her kids running and playing and outside.

At this time the family still lived about 3 miles from the nearby rail road crossing. Mother's garden was still flourishing in the spring and summer months. All the children would follow a path that led down the rail road tracks to greet the workers the train with a hearty smile and big friendly wave! The workers would throw pennies and candy out to us as the train drifted down the lonesome trail!

The kids wore mostly hand me downs clothes fashioned from the trash cans of America's thrown away treasures. Father collected pretty dresses, skirts, blouses, pants, shoes, purses, and sometimes a few trinkets of sparkling earrings and shiny necklaces on his daily job routes. We were happy to get all those wonderful trinkets! Everyone churches admired mother's lovely newly and classic attire not knowing that her fashionable wardrobe had come from the city dump! Our home was furnished from this upscale neighborhood as well! There was fine lace curtains that hung in the living room, sofas, chairs, beds, lamps, and kitchen appliances too! Walter knew how to make needed repairs to worn out electrical cords and fix broken furniture legs. Marie scrubbed her knuckles to the bone hand washing dirty sofa covers until they were sparkling clean like new.

Although the four room shack was old and faded out building with remnants of rusted nails and rotten planks it's insides were filled with all of Walter's golden trinkets that he had collected to make his family more comfortable terrible times of poverty and lack!

A bunch of wild yellow buttercup tulips sprang up around the door steps. In the spring and summer Marie filled the house with vases of pretty colored snap dragons lovely wild red roses. The windows and

Generation Bloodline The Survival of Life

doors opened up to allow the sweet fragrances to flow thru every room in the house.

Winter was beautiful and cold. Snow and ice transformed the old house into an exquisite portrait of a big old ice castle. Walter started a brimming setback fire in the fireplace to warm his kids frost bitten feet. He worked hard sun up and sun down swinging his mighty axe and splitting logs to keep and ample supply on hand to keep the home fires burning all through the night.

Walter was desperate and determined opponent in the game of survival of life and defeat poverty and death. His greatest possessions in life were his wife and children! The storms of life scorched his hands and feet with painful calluses as he swung his axe back and forth while the cold wind defend his frozen ears! Yet, through all the pain and suffering, his loyalty and devotions for his family never wavered and remained strong to sustain his world

Having so many children, sickness was always right around the corner. One year Marie's little daughter Mary endured a brutal attack of rheumatic fever and whooping cough! She was a small and sickly child that always got the worsted of any ordeal! For three long weeks she lingered on the brink of death, throwing up every morsel of food that she swallowed. Even though Marie was nine months pregnant, night after night she walked back and forth on the floor, cradling her child's frail body in her arms! She prayed night and day to God asking him to heal her poor sick baby! Walter and Marie had almost given up hope for her recovery!

With her pupils dilated and her small skeletal frame teetered on a thin line between life and deaf! Sorrowful tears streamed down her sad face as she wept for her baby! Little Mary's illness had put tremendous pressures upon her tired shoulders! Marie defiantly remained by her bedside comforting her through the bouts of hacking coughs and grasps for air as she clung thru a thin line of hope!

Miraculously, little Mary had survived to the next morning and was sitting up in bed with her eyes wide opened! God had heard and answered a mother's prayers! Everyone came running into the bedroom whey they heard their mother shouting praises up to the heavens, thanking Almighty God for his tender mercies and wonderful miracles that he had delivered on that wonderful blessed morning! The whole entire family was happy and thanking that little Mary had made it through a severe crisis and on the mends to make a full recovery! They all sat around the crackling fire and sang gospel songs that night before retiring to bed!

After surviving rheumatic fever and whooping cough, the road to recovery was a very Logan difficult journey for little Mary! The horrendous effects of her illness left her unable to walk! Her limbs were weak and brittle! Her face had transformed to a slender hallow shape with bulging eyes! She had learn to crawl before ever thinking about walking again

As time passed, Mary grew strong enough to raise up on her all fours and crawl to her mother! Deliriously happy, Marie jumped to her feet and did a holy ghost dance! She declared in Jesus's name that her baby would soon walk again!

Marie was so relieved that the hardest part of the battle to save her child was over! But now, she had to prepare to bear the laboring pains to bring another new life into the world!

Everyone was exhausted from doing clean up details under father's military instructions and ready for a needed break. Suddenly, Marie was fiercely awakened by a sharp hard stabbing pain in her gut! She looked down and saw that her water had broke and saturated her gown with it's warm fluids! In a panic state she yelled for Walter to come quickly to her aide! He rushed into the room and wrapped her in a soft blanket. Then helped her get into the car and took her to Doctor's Hammonds office.

Father was proud his fine automobile! It was a black Fleet Line Slope Back Chevrolet that he had purchased out of the yard of one of his clients during trash detail and made necessary edging repairs. He was hoping that Marie would not have their baby in his pretty shiny black car!

Doctor Hammonds was the best doctor for colored folk in Butts County. He and his dutiful nurse Dora Maddox had delivered many healthy babies into the world. Marie knew she would receive the very best care possible. Lingering and suffering thru several hours of riveting labor pains, finally, her new baby was born. Marie was so happy and relieved to have delivered a beautiful healthy baby girl. Her little bundle of joy was fully equipped with all her fingers and toes. Walter beamed with pride and joy as he held his baby girl in his arms for the first time.

Living on the poor side of town offered a few escape routes from the boring and mundane routines of everyday life. There were hardly any club outlets or entertainment facilities available. Young folk usually attended sporting events at the High School or enjoyed a country picnic. Some would sip on a dollar shot of home brew at a back woods juke joint. Others attended church services to beg for forgiveness of their fleshy sins of folly.

Walter and Marie were very religious in their own way. Every Sunday the girls would put on their prettiest dresses and jump in the back seat of their farther's old Fleet Line Chevrolet. They anxiously awaited for the rest of the family to join them. Then they would head out to the morning devotion at church. The knucklehead boys would be tussling and arguing over which one of them was going to sit by the window. The oldest sister Mahalia would thump them in the head and tell them to behave before on of them fall out of the car. To make them settle down, she would make funny clown faces and they would all burst out laughing. There were so many kids piled up in the backseat that there were not enough seat belts to go around. The smaller kids would sit in the laps of the bigger kids. They were packed tightly together like sardines in a can.

Reverend Wright, the Pastor of the United Pentecostal Church, was a very tall and stone faced man. If he looked at you without cracking a friendly smile, you better get outta the way cause he was going to pour out fire and brimstone with his loud stern sermons. He stood proudly as he preached the word of the gospel. The sisters in the church were mesmerized by his tall handsome frame. Every time he spoke their hearts caught on fire with the Holy Spirit. Causing them to leap from their seats and perform a holy dance. They exhausted themselves until they fell to the floor and spoke in tongues. The mystical presence of the Holy Spirit was so potent that it stirred up the congregation to explode in a thunderous declaration of praise and worship to Almighty God!

Whenever there was a new member to join the church, the entire congregation assembled in the middle of the sanctuary and surrounded the secret pool as it arose from underneath the pulpit. Mothers, daughters, fathers, and sons stood side by side hand in hand dressed in pure white gowns without wrinkles or blemishes singing, "Take Me to the Water to be baptized!" The pastor's gown floated on top of the deep waters as he bowed his head a second time to signal the female saints to stand at alert for any emergencies that may occur during the Holy baptism. A third and final bow permitted the deacons to escort the newcomer to join him inside the glistening flowing waters. The church assembly raised their hands and chanted an old familiar negro spiritual song that was highly regarded in their hearts. Deacon Wilson escorted the newcomer to the center of the pool. Holding him arm in arm on each side, he and Pastor Wright lowered the newcomer underneath the waters while reciting a prophetic scripture from the book of proverbs. Grasping for air as he rose to the surface of the pool. He wiped away the stinging water from his burning eyes and yelled, "Thank You Jesus!" After the completion of the annunciation, the newcomer rested in the deacon's chambers while the others prepared for a grand celebration.

CHAPTER 9

LIFE OR DEATH

NOVEMBER 23, 1963

Walter's favorite relaxing place was an old tree stump out in the back yard. He would take a sip of white lightening from an old jelly jar then, fill his jaw with a plug sweet chewing tobacco. He said it would chase the flies and mosquitos away. Little Mary would run and jump in his lap and listen to all his funny and scary fairy tales. As the two enjoyed the cool breeze, He would laugh and tell his baby girl, "You're gonna break some man's heart some day when you look at him with those cute puppy dog eyes and say good bye! But if he's not treating you right or making you cry, drop his low down cheating self so quick that it will make his head spend! Baby girl, I want you to always be brave and never fear anything or anybody! You are going to grow up to be strong and beautiful. You can melt the coldest heart with those beautiful eyes of yours!

It was a cold brisk morning when father got up to make a big warm set back fire before going to work. He placed his work boots in front of the fireplace and hurried to the kitchen to fix his lunch! Little Mary was awakened by the popping logs on top of the red hot coals as they caught a blaze. She could see smoke coming from Walter's boots as they dried from the warmth of the flames. The smell of her mother's sweet potato pie coming from the kitchen filled the air. Mary called out to her father but no one answered. She thought maybe he had already left for work, but still wondered why his boots were still sitting in front of the fire?

She snuck from underneath the covers and tipped into the kitchen to swipe a slice of her mother's delicious pie, and when she returned to the room, her father's boots had mysteriously disappeared into thin air. Nibbling at the pilfered treat, she became afraid and jumped back into the bed and hid underneath the covers.

Snuggling closer to her mother, she put her head under the covers and settled down for a restful sleep. Marie got up to tend to the burning flames, making sure that all the sparks and hot coils were safely retained inside the fire place. She checked the wicks in the kerosene lamps too. With the assurance that all was well, she blew out the flames in the lamps and returned to her bed.

The roosters with tall red cones standing on top of their heads cackled "Cock-a-doodle-do!" And announced the brand new day. Slowly the sun rose to light up the skies and awaken the sleepy kids and letting them know that it was time to get up and start morning chores. Suddenly they were stopped in their tracks by a strange knock at the door. Marie opened the door to find Mr Tingle with a sorrowful look on his face. His voice was trembling as he cleared his throat and said, "I am sorry to be the bearer of this sad news Mrs Lawrence, but, your husband is dead! He was crushed to death by an on coming train! His car was totally demolished in the accident as well!" Marie fell to the floor in riving pain and moaning agonizing tears! Her heart had just been ripped from her chest from hearing the devastating news that the love of her life was dead!

Marie screamed from the top of her lungs, "No God Please No! Please Jesus, don't take him from me! This cannot be true! Who is gonna help me feed and take care of all these kids? Oh My God, How will I be able to feed all these kids and keep a roof over our heads?

Their hearts ached as they watched their mother fell to the floor in moanful groans of sorrow! The family clung to each other for strength to survive the loss of their beloved father! The next few days were very difficult for Marie. She felt as though she was still asleep and not able to awake from a horrible nightmare. Over the next few days, friends, family and neighbors visited the house to pay their respects to Walter and his family. Some relatives came to offer condolences to the family, but others came to steal anything that wasn't nailed to the floor. They locked the kids outside of the kitchen. Then loaded up boxes of food and carried it too their cars! Aunt Lillie Mae was the main culprit in the big food heist. She was telling the ladies to make haste before someone discovered their dastardly deed.

It was later rumored that Walter had been brutally murdered by a racist mob and his lifeless body returned to his car and driven onto the railroad tracks to cover up the horrible crime! Some people in the town had also spread gossip that Walter's wife Marie was a white woman and this rumor may have cost him his life! By infuriating the Caucasian community into a murderous racist mob into becoming their own judge and jury and taking an innocent life!

Marie's oldest son Walt Jr worked for a local farmer named Mr Bass. While working in the barn, he overheard his employer and some of his friends bragging about how they had surprised his father Walter outside of his car one morning and beat him to death! They had ordered him to go quietly or they would kill everybody in the house! This horrible truth would lay buried in time for over twenty years until Walt Jr revealed it to his sister Mary as they stood at the foot of their father's grave on Father's Day!

The funeral felt so unreal! Marie and her children wanted no part in this awful tragedy unfolding in the center stage of their lives! The morning was cold and wet. The entire family was overcome with a great sense of loss and sadness! As time to review the body of the dearly beloved family member for the last time arrived, Marie began to shake all over as she looked upon Walter's face! The very thought of her husband's lifeless body resting motionless in the coffin tore her heart to pieces as she pleaded for him to wake up from his deathly sleep!

Suddenly the vessels in Marie's head began to beat like loud marching drums. Everything in the church began swinging back and forth. All she could see was Walter's face smiling back at her in a trance as she fainted at the head of his casket. The ushers picked her up and carried her outside to catch some fresh air. The kids followed closely behind her and circled each other with a strong hug!

Life without her Walter was like living in an unfinished painting! So many unexplored facets of raw emotions left to grey colorless times!

There was no more laughter! No more kisses or warm arms to cling to on those cold bitter nights!

During the summer of 1964, Marie took her family to work with her into the cotton fields. Each child had a certain amount of cotton to pick. The children considered the task at hand as a competitive game. They enjoyed racing up and down the long rows of snow bulbs as they were jokingly called! They paid no attention to the sun's hot rays blaring down on their heads. The money they earned, helped to put a little more food on the table. Marie also took in laundry from old lady Cleveland who lived farther down the rail road tracks.

Purchasing a few small chicks from the local hardware store, she raised them to cackling hens that produced fresh eggs and good old fried chicken for Sunday Dinner. Mr Lambert, the cotton farmer came to the house everyday to pick up all the field hands to work on his farm. His truck was so loud and noisy that you could hear all the nuts and bolts clinking and rattling for miles down the road.

Marie and the kids grabbed their straw hats and lunch pales and jumped on back of the truck and headed for the cotton fields. Walt Jr cracked a few jokes to pass the time as he watched out for the younger kids, making sure they did not slip or fall off the back of the truck. He would tell them once to sit down, and next time he would smack them good and sit them down in a safe area while the truck was still in motion. Once they arrived at the fields, he helped them off the truck and handed them their nap sacks and told them to work as fast as they could to fill them up and come back for more bags to fill.

At lunch break, they all walked back to the rear of the truck where they stood in line to get a cool drink of water and buy some snacks from Mr. Lambert if they had not brought snacks from home! When they finally got home, their clothes would be drenched with sweat and dirt. Their shoes were left to air out on the porch before they went inside to take a bath in an old wash tub.

Years after Walter's death, The Railroad Company paid a small settlement to Marie which allowed her and her family to move to McDonough GA in 1965. Walt Jr bought his first car at 17 years of age. It was a blue and white fifty-six Chevrolet. Every time he took his brothers and sisters for a ride, you could hear his favorite song "Love

Potion Number Nine" flowing out the speakers. As years passed, he as well as several other family members left the nest venture out on their own, leaving the smaller kids behind to adjust to an ever changing future.

CHAPTER 10

MARY ATTENDS A NEW SCHOOL

Every day of School, I walked into the arena as a brave little soldier and faced my fellow classmates who had vial wicked infested tongues of snakes! They were filled with hate and jealousy and deadly claws that ripped my self esteem and confidence right out of my chest!

Walking in the centerline of neutrality, I was too black to be white and too white to be black! I was called half breed or white girl as I walked down the hallway heading to class. The school library became a sanctuary. Books became my closest friends. I was in control and could turn the pages and read about faraway places to fill the lonely echoes of silence.

One day as I was walking down to the lunch cafeteria, I heard some sweet soul music blaring from the back door entrance of the gymnasium. Curious to know where it was coming from and who was playing the music, I peaked outside and looked up into the tall tower overlapping the Foot Ball Field where I saw the prettiest and smartest girls in West Side High School. With their stylish cut bangs, bell bottom jeans and mini skirts, Frances, Mary Jane and Sandra, The Bell sisters were spinning all those solid gold hits from Motown. I could see they were having a ball up there, popping gum. snapping their fingers and swinging their bodies from side to side, dancing to that unforgettable hit by the Intruders, called; Cowboys And Girls.

I snuck out on to the ball fielding started dancing like I was in a broadway show! When they saw me spinning, twisting and doing the funky chicken and four corners dancing, the girls let out a roaring laugh and started cheering me on! Aww yeah this little girl to git down. I did a turn around and spin, slid to the side, humped my shoulders left and right! Then, rotated my body all the way down to the ground and back up again.

The gym teacher noticed me and waited until I finished my dance then she dragged me by my arm back to class. All the while she was telling me, ok Lawrence, since you so energetic and limber, lets see how fast you can run out here on the basket ball court.

Glimpsing from the corner of my eyes I could see the Bell sisters laughing as I was being led off the field. Then their other sister Georgia yelled, "Hey little girl, come back tomorrow at lunch and dance for us again! You are a good dancer!"

DECEMBER 18, 1970

It was Christmas time. I was Twelve years old. Everyone at school had the Christmas spirit. Teachers passed out Peppermint canes and boxes of chocolate covered cherry candies to their favorite students. Pretty colored decorations were displayed on the hallway bulletin board. A tall tree adorned with blue and gold ornaments and blinking lights was show cased in the front office. Giddy laughter and chatter filled the halls every time the bell ranged between classes. You might catch a glimpse of some love struck sappy boy holding a bunch of mistletoe over his sweetheart's head and trying to steal a kiss! I even heard a chorus of Jingle Bells floating in the air.

With all those jovial shenanigans going on, I still harbored a lonely and restless spirit. My first puppy love crush and I had had a heated argument that led to us going our separate ways. I was heart broken at the thought of never seeing him again! He was in Junior class, older and more experienced in life than I was. Why do some idiots break up with their girlfriends on Christmas just to keep from buying a simple gift? I would have been happy to receive a homemade holiday card or listen to him sing me a sweet love song.

Billy was 16 years of age and had a wild streak of adventure under his hat. He had hinted about wanting to have sex with me on several occasions. I wondered if he was angry with me because I said no to his demands for sexual pleasures. He kept telling me that he had a great burning desire burning below his belt that needed to be satisfied. Then he would place my hand near the zipper of his pants and tell me to stroke his bulging penis. I would remove my hand and shyly back away from him! All this sex stuff was too much for me to understand. I had never had sex with anyone in my entire young life. A kiss and a hug yes, but, that was as far as I had explored.

A scrumptious aroma greeted me as I approached the doorway of the family home. As usual, mom was baking Christmas cakes for the holiday feast. Avoiding any confrontation, I quickly walked through the kitchen and to my room. Upon entering my bedroom, my body instantaneously began shake! Perspiration poured Downey cheeks as if I had a fever. I was overwhelmed by suffocating heat all over my body! What was wrong, I wondered? I laid on the bed and fell asleep.

Several hours later, Billy dropped by for a visit. My heart danced when I looked into his eyes! He was my everything! Blinded by the love bug, I did not realize that he was still angry at me because I had refused to sleep with him. I felt so ashamed because I was a virgin and did not know how to make love and satisfy his desires.

Several days earlier, I had caught him and my best friend Verna making out in back of the High School. Verna was more experienced in sexual intimacy, her reputation as a wild child was well known. The two of them were locked in a passionate embrace when I stumbled upon their heated love fest. Clearing my throat to get their attention, I laughed and walked away! I didn't want them to know how badly my heart was aching inside! I could hardly bear the sight of their lustful betrayal that cut deep inside my soul! My whole body was drenched in aching pain and agony! But I was not going to let them see me shed not one tear!

I wanted to mend the fences between us so I eagerly agreed to go to the movies with Billy. I found it odd though that he was going in the direction opposite the movie theatre. Maybe he knows a short cut, I thought.

When the car stopped, the only scenery visible were the stars overhead and the blackness of night covering everything else. Billy pulled me closer to hime and began caressing my breasts. I tried to free myself from his clutches but was unsuccessful! I knew nothin at all about sex and was nervous as a cat. Billy became a ferocious savage beast he tore my top opened and lowered his head and began sucking my nipples. He then ripped off my clothing and flung me back onto the seat and plunged his big hard dick inside of my vagina! Tears showered down my bruised face as I begged and pleaded for him to stop ! How could suck a violent and painful attack be called love? The more I struggled the more he jabbed his oversized penis into my bleeding pussy!

Then from out of the shadowy darkness, his friend Wilbert appeared. While calling out for help, Billy grabbed my hands and pulled me out of the car and threw me onto the cold ground! He told Wilbert to To come and get him some pussy too! Blinking in and out of consciousness, I suffered through five hours of being repeatedly raped by These two mean and evil guys! Wilbert bit my clitoris with his teeth so hard until I was raw and swollen!

At 12 AM in the morning, Billy and Wilbert decided they had enough and were done with me! Billy started started choking me and throwing my into the bushes! Crawling on my knees, I kept pleading for my life and promising not to tell anyone about the incident! Billy yelled, "Naw bitch! Verna was gonna give me all the loving I wanted and needed the other day, but you messed that up didn't you! Payback is a mother fucker!"

Wilbert grabbed Billy by his arms and pulled him off top of me! He shook him and said, "Man you know this shit aint' right! I don't want no part in killing this girl! We have done too much to her as it is! She says she will not tell on us, so, let's just drop her off and get the hell out of here right now!"

Billy finally agreed to take me home. Before I got out of the car, Billy gave me a crystal ball with a replica of Santa Claus, his sleigh and tiny reindeers all covered in snow flakes. The crystal was beautiful, but it was not enough to erase the ugly and despicable and brutal acts that they had tortured my mind body and soul with! I felt utter shame and disgust and blamed myself for being so young and dumb! Upon exiting the vehicle, I yelled, "Burn in hell you dirty low down dogs!" The innocence of love was forever destroyed and never to rise in my heart again! I felt so nasty and dirty like I wasn't worth anything, no more than dirt and rocks on the ground!

The holidays came to festive end for everyone else but me. Vacation time was over for all the students, so we all knuckled down and hit the books to earn the required credits for promotion to higher grade level.

My first period class was English. The teacher's assignment for that day was to write an essay about our activities during the holiday season. I sat quietly staring at a blank piece of paper, wondering what to write? I could see Billy walking in the hallway with his new girlfriend Vera. For some odd reason, I guess he was still trying to hurt me. I could hear them snickering and joking around! The laughter became louder until I just couldn't take it any longer! Crying hysterically, I leaped from my seat and ran down the hall to the girl's bathroom!

I had calmed down at lunch time went to my filth period science class. My assignment was to cut open and dissect the inside of a frog. All my props were set up for demonstration when Vera came strutting inside the classroom carrying a note from Billy. Opening the note, I began reading the mean spirited words. They read as follows; "You no good tramp! I don't want you no more! I love Vera, she don't mind pleasing her man! Stay away from means my future wife. You nasty stinking whore!

I was speechless and paralyzed with fear anger and disgusted at Billy's cruel harsh words! My teacher Ms. Combs noticed hesitation in my demonstration and asked, what's the hold up Mary? Noticing the note clinched in my hand, she confiscated it and silently read its contents. In utter disgust, she yelled,

Vera don't come up in here passing rude notes and disturbing my class! You and Billy go strait to the Principal's office right now! Vera wiped that smirking smile off her face and scooted out the door.

Mrs Combs said to Mary, I don't know what's wrong, but if there is anything that you need, please let me know! You're a fine student! I am proud of your work! Continue on with your demonstration, she won't bother you anymore! She and Billy are cooling their heels in the Principal's Office!

I was tormented and humiliated in front of my classmates by Billy's new girlfriend, Vera! She was the stuck up jealous type that wanted all eyes focused on her. Vera was a real mean girl with a nasty attitude and wicked laugher. She would stand in the hallway and hurl snarling insults at me with her evil tongue and tear my heart to pieces! I cringed and dropped my head in shame every time she and Billy came near me!

I remember once, going outside the back door of my home and standing outside in the thunder and rain trying to wash away Billy's nasty finger prints from my skin! Even the lightening flashing a blaze across the skies could not shed light upon my bleak and darkened world! I was like a shadow case upon the ground, a mere image of hopelessness! Even though hard the blistering rain covered my body, it was not enough to remove the awful stain and pain in my heart!

I could no longer feel any compassion for anything or anybody! All the walls of love and trust had been forever shattered into bits and pieces of glass and cut deeply into my soul! And left only sores of pain and agony wherever it saw fit!

The brutal attack and forceful submission to a deranged and demented maniac in a tirade of vengeful rage and unbridled sexual attack stole my virginity and innocence and rendered me a helpless victim! My body was battered and bruised from the top of my head to the soles of my feet! My pussy was torn, swollen and bleeding, my feet were sore from being dragged and then thrown into the bushes! How could Billy say he loved me with one breath, and then beat the tar out me with his angry fists? If this is what he called love, then I wanted no part of it!

With only one mind and one voice, how could I heal and free myself from this deep festering memory that held me captive in a horrific nightmare of uncontrollable pain and mental anguish?

I wanted to speak out and tell someone about what Billy and his friend had done to me, but, fear silenced my thoughts and hindered me from telling my mother or anyone else in authority! I was ashamed and didn't want mother to think that I was a bad girl and that it was my own fault that I got raped! She would asked me why I was afraid to open the windows or go outside? And also why I cried late into the night alone in my room? The anxiety that I felt was so strong, it would start at the bottom my back and travel upwards to my throat and render me speechless! Every night before I closed my eyes, I would softly hum some soothing words, Gotta Find Me An Angel To Fly Away With Me! Gotta Find Me An Angel To Set Me Free! Then one night the most beautiful angel with the most beautiful eyes as pretty as the clear blue skies, and shiny golden locks of hair that floated in the air, came to my bedside and asked me why was I so sad! I blinked my eyes three times and she faded into thin air! I then closed my eyes and drifted into a most peaceful sleep!

Mary became withdrawn and spent countless hours in the school library to avoid any further confrontations with Billy and his nasty girl friend Vera. It was in that same library that she found and abundance of friends that could not bring any harm to her because they were written characters on the many pages of the many books that she would read every day. The words in print cold not lie or betray her as so many other people had done in her past. She was in complete control. All she had to do was open the book of her choice, turn the pages and read until she was satisfied!

During the completion of high School, Mary 's intelligence increased tremendously. She was not very well liked by her classmates because of frequent high test scores on all semester examinations. She was targeted as a smart ass brat and called spiteful names like white girl or half breed. If only these kids knew the loneliness she felt in her heart, surely they would have been more kind and friendly to her! She often felt abandoned by everyone and had no one to confide in or find comfort!

Locked away in her room and staring out of her window, with tears running down her cheeks, she searched the pillars her soul to find peace and contentment once again! Mary feared that if she told her mother about being assaulted that she would bring shame on her entire family! So she carried the weight of guilt upon her shoulders for years to come!

Living in a fantasy world created in her mind, she became the ruler of her own destiny! No one could ever hurt her again. She thanked God that she did not get pregnant from the brutal assault by Billy and His friend Wilbert!

CHAPTER 11A

CAPTIVE OF MY HEART PART 1

AUGUST 23, 1974

After Graduation, Mary became weary of the fantasy world that she had created. Day after day, she sat on the porch watching her life drift through time! On a long hot summer's day, she noticed a white station wagon passing in front of the house. She decided that very moment that the person driving in that car was going to be her prince charming coming to free her from her imaginary world. At last, she was going to break free from her make believe world and step into a real world with real people!

As he neared the mail box, with a sexy walk in her step, Mary strolled down to the end of the driveway and across the street to the mail box. Slamming on his brakes in the middle of the road, he jokingly said, what are you doing out here stopping all this traffic! What may I ask is your name pretty Lady? Mary smiled and turned to walk back across the street, when suddenly he leaped from his car, grabbed her hands and escorted her back to her driveway.

For an instance we became the only inhabitants on earth! Their surroundings were transformed into a garden of paradise! Mary was overwhelmed by his good smelling cologne! Roses appeared to fall at her feet as he gazed wildly into her eyes. She was enchanted by his big beautiful eyes.

Please forgive me pretty lady, may I introduce myself? My name is Daren Tate, he proudly acknowledged. May I ask, what is your name? Let me guess, is it Patricia or Victoria? No, those names don't fit this lovely face ! Hum? My mother's name is Mary. Is this your name too? Yes, that's it! I see you blushing. Very glad to meet you Mary!

He noticed that she was a bit nervous by his presence, so he began talking about himself. I've been visiting McDonough for about three months now, going back and forth to the gymnasium for work out practice. Basket ball is a hobby of mine. Maybe you might like to comets the gym and watch me play with the team sometimes, huh? I really would love to see you out there in the bleachers cheering me on! May I come and visit with you again next week? I would love for you to meet my family!

Now tell me beautiful lady, what are you doing out here showing off those sexy legs? You should be flooded with admirers! His flirtatious boldness made her heart dance with delight! He was as cunning as a fox with a silver tongue, knowing exactly what to say to get what he wanted. Oh my goodness, I knew you had a lovely smile to match that lovely face of yours, he said.

Mary didn't know whether he was serious or just kidding around with her? After pleading to take her out to dinner and a movie, she finally agreed dinner at a nearby restaurant called Sizzling Platter. The following afternoon, she was surprised to see that he was so punctual. Their laughter filled the air as they munched out on a delicious T Bone Steak, salad and baked potato. The glass of red wine was a soothing and warmed them over right down to the tips of their toes.

Comfortable and relaxed, they felt as though they had known each therefor an eternity! The evening ended at a run down motel. The condition of the room, however, did not put a damper on their raw erotic emotions. An intoxicating aroma blossomed like wild flowers as the two star crossed lovers embraced!

Daron softly whispered in her ear and said, you are a timeless piece of pure joy and pleasure and virtual tapestry of priceless treasure! I long to be one with such an extraordinary specimen of magnificent beauty! Let me hold you closely to my heart and full fill your innermost needs and desires! I see the passion sparkling deep within your soul. Your eyes twinkle like the stars in the night sky! Let me lay my head onto your breasts of soft pillars as I bow to your every command. I need your love so desperately! Please say that you'll be mine forever!

Mary sweetly replied, What a rare and precious diamond I have found among sand and stone! You are the man of my dreams! How I long to be swept up into your big strong loving arms! Your sweet words of desire seamy hearten fire with a blazing hot inferno of wild passion fires! I surrender all to you and only you my love!

Daren grabbed Mary's trembling hand and planted a gentle kiss in her palm. She could feel his hot bated breath all over her body as he stroked her forehead and began kissing her ever so tenderly from her head to her feet! Reaching his favorite spot on her quivering body, he begnnibbling on her hot, wet, and juicy vagina, searching for clusters of hidden passions! Her body vibrated fiercely as he teased every part with his stinging tongue! Holding her buttocks tightly in the palms of his hands, he pushed his way deeper into her womb! Mary declared to her beloved Daren, "you are a pleasure dome of endless rapture! I cling to your arms and ride with waves of desire and reach complete culmination and burn brightly as embers from a hot wild fire!

At last Mary had realized that love between a man and a woman was not brutal or painful! Daron had erased the awful memory of her being violated and raped by Billy and Wilbert. Love was fresh new and wonderful! She was no longer afraid to give part of herself to the man that had set her free from a world of endless nightmares!

Love struck, Mary was unable to seethe real Daren hidden behind the mask of darkness! The cost she paid for a fleeting moment of love and happiness was way too high! Liked a captured bird with clipped wings, she would fall victim to his jealous tirades and become his battered prey!

Daren was a very intriguing man, full of bizarre and adventurous treachery! His strange, bondage love and possessive and controlling ways were very well camouflaged behind those big brown eyes and bright shinning grin! There were many red flags, but Mary's nose was so wide opened that a whole truck load of bull shit could come thru it without her ever noticing or getting out of the way! Strong out and head over heals, she was a fool in love!

Daron pleaded for her to accompany him to his sister's home and maybe even live there together until they were able to get an apartment. She wrestled with herself trying to make a decision coming down heavy.

It reminded her of little Indians doing a war dance as the droplets touched the puddles floating on the ground.

She felt like a kid anxiously awaiting a Christmas when she saw him coming down the driveway of her home! Though she had not yet decided to make the move to the big city with Daron, she greeted him with opened arms.

Placing one foot before the other, she decided catch the 4 P.M. bus leaving for the big city with Daron. Before leaving she told her mother of her decision to move to the big city with Daron. "Mama I love him! He makes me feel so alive! For a long time now I have hated myself and hated men because I thought that love was dirty and nasty! Daron showed me that Love is wonderful, soft and gentle! I have got to go where love leads me to go!"

After a long sigh, her mother began to speak. "Well, Mary, you're eighteen years old now, but, you'll always be my little girl. I've watched you everyday sitting the same place gazing out into the streets and never going out or having any friends. It hurts me to see you so lonely and never smiling. I don't know what happened to you to destroy your trust in people, but if Daron makes you happy, I will not stop you from leaving home! Please take care of yourself and call me and let me know how you are doing up there in the big city!

With her mother's blessing, Mary started packing for the trip to Atlanta. Anticipation gripped her soul as She and Daron toured the city while riding the bus. She was disappointed to see the buildings were not as large as she remembered as a child. It seemed as though she had been living in a dream world. The colors of the city, the image of Atlanta being a grand and large castle sealed in a bubble was only a mirage. Riding the bus they passed luxury apartments on the rich side of town. At the end of their destination, they stood in front of a crumbling complex. Rats as big as cats roamed the streets as though they were part of the neighborhood. The people were raggedly dressed, bumming nickels and dimes to buy cigarettes and cheap wine. Grown men sitting on the corner begging for pennies made me sick to my stomach to see their pitiful existence of a degrading life.

The entire area was a dilapidated slum! Mary was on the poorest side of town. She never imagined in her wildest dreams that Atlanta with all its tall buildings and plush offices, expensively dressed patrons, would also house an unmentionable part of the city where people were crowded in tiny government apartments, bunched up like baby chicks running around in a chicken coop!

She was stuck again in an unsightly predicament, a prisoner of an impoverished neighborhood of was so overwhelmed with despair about her living situation but refused to go back home to her mother! She loved Daron with every fiber of her being and decided to give their love a chance against all odds!

His sisters were very nice! They got along very well. Daron's sister Betty's children, Sheila, Boo Boo, Sheri and Stanley became very close and bonded as a family. Daron became insanely jealous of their family alliance. Not wanting to put a strain on their troublesome relationship, Mary agreed to move to an apartment three buildings down from his sister's home.

She assumed the issue had been resolved, until Daron began questioning her about her daily routine while he was away at work. He would check the dishes in the sink, her shoes, clothes, her breath, and even sniffed her panties! Mary became weary of Daron's constant interrogations and felt like a prisoner in her own home! She had no rights as an adult except performing her marital duties in the bedroom! Daron had become very demanding and controlling, he told her what to wear, what books to read, what programs to watch on Television. He saw watched her dolling up her face in the mirror and accused her of making herself pretty for another man. Why didn't he realize that every woman wants to feel pretty to bolster her inward confidence and self esteem! He became so angry that he smeared lip stick all over her face and drew clown lips on her face, then shoved her face hard into the mirror while laughing and joking about how ugly she looked!

Sometimes he would go into the kitchen, open up the cabinet doors and rearrange all the labels on the cans the way he thought they should be arranged. If the food was not to his prepared to his specifications, he would throw it out the back door! If he was late for supper and the food was cold, he demanded Mary to cook more food! He had become a brute and selfish bastard!

Mary clung to Daron like wall paper trying to conceal the painful scars of their thrills and spills through good times and bad times! Daron had forgotten that Mary needed to be loved, nurtured, and most of all deserved his loyalty, devotion and compassion too!

Their love dwindled to the pages of yesterday's dust and slowly faded away. The relationship became one of a competitive sport. If Mary won a simple game of spade, Daren wold get so riled up and catch a case of the black ass, and be down right so rude and nasty that no one on earth could get along with him! He put Mary through pure torture and hell with his outrageous rantings until he was satisfied that she had been punished!

SEPTEMBER 1976

Even with the birth of their first child, he never let up from his demanding and controlling ways! He was jealous of his own son that Mary carried in her belly! She was eight months pregnant and didn't feel like traveling or visiting friends. Daren insisted that Mary go with him to visit his friends John and Marsha who lived way across town. They would have to catch the bus to get to their home. While they were traveling on the bus, Daren accuse Mary of looking at some guy that she had never met before! A heated argument came to a boiling point as they exited the bus. Walking across the street to the park, the cars speeded up and down the highway like they were riding on racing tracks. Daren was watching zoom by and accused the passing strangers of flashing hand and light signals to Mary. Tired of the on going interrogation, Mary started cowardly looking down at the ground while holding Daren's in order to avoid any contact with the passing motorists!

Daren went stark raving mad with paranoia! For a second, Mary saw herself running in front of theca's to end her torment from this foolish monster! He kept demanding, bitch, you gonna tell me what the hell is going on or I will choke the last breath of life from your weak ass mind! Smile bitch! Act like you love everything that I am telling you! You better not shed one tear! I will scrub your pretty face into the sidewalk and stomp you all the way into China!

Mary heart began to beat faster and fosters we arrived at Daren's friends home. She managed to muster up a faint smile and pretended that everything was ok. With a quick knock at the door, Marsha greeted and welcomed us to come inside. She greeted them with a fake come inside. Though she smiled on the outside, she could not hide her cold and devious heart. Her husband John was a tall slender man full of trickery and mischief! He was aware of Daren's insane jealousy towards Mary and constantly pushed his buttons. At one point, John asked Mary if she would like to dance with him? She could feel Daren's eyes flare up as John pulled her close to his chest and laughingly joked, hey man, nobody can dance with Mary like me! He twirled Mary around and dipped her into his arms as they danced to the sweet music on the radio!

Mary was unaware that Marsha and Daren had dated before she and John had gotten married. John had some issues about this fact and was trying to get back at Daren for laying pipe to his old lady with Daren's emotions! With friends like these two, who needs more enemies?

After Daren took Mary home, he beat the living tar out of her! With gorilla strength he snatched cord from the iron and tied her hands behind her back, shoved her to the floor, then spat in her face while pulling her hair! He pulled her by her hair again, slammed her to the floor and began stomping and kicking her with his big feet! Daren yelled, I'm gonna break you down to nothing! Do you hear me! You aint' shit bitch!

In total fear, Mary begged and pleaded for her life! "Please don't hurt me anymore! Marsha and John are your friends. I don't know why they are playing games with you like this? I love you!

Lighting a cigarette, he smiled wickedly with every puff. He tore off Mary's clothes, climbed on top of her shivering naked body! Mary screamed in pain and agony as he stuck the hot burning cigarette to her vagina! He yelled, you working for the mafia, aint' you bitch? You trying to kill me, aint you bitch!

Mary anxiously replied, that's not true! You are crazy! Daren looked into her eyes with a mean and angry look on his face like he was possessed by some kind of evil monster! Frozen in her steps Mary didn't know what to next expect? Grabbing her in the collar, he began to slap her face from one side to the other!

Mary tried to calm him down by asking what was wrong? She continuously pleaded for him to stop his vicious attack against her bruised and battered body! "Daren please tell me what did I do wrong? Tell me now and I won't ever do it again!

Daren yelled, you lying bitch! I saw you looking at John! Don't fuck over me! Mary replied, I would never cheat on you with your friend John!

Daren grew tired from beating up on Mary's ass and went into the bedroom and fell asleep. Unable to move, she laid there on the floor starring up at the lights in the ceiling, constantly asking herself what the hell was wrong with this maniac? She could shea shadowy image reaching out to her! With its winged like arms, it picked her from the floor, touched her neck with his feathered wings and she could move again! Motioning with its stretched out wings, it pointed to the door and motioned for her to run out of the door! Who was this heavenly creature that absorbed her pain and helped her get back up on her feet?

Thinking inwardly, she decided to make her daring escape and leave Daren! She knew that if she didn't leave, the situation would only get worse with more deadly consequences! Slowly she crept to the doorway while glancing to the bedroom to see if evil Daren was still asleep? Taking off her shoes, she then tipped out the door and ran as fast as she could to freedom!

Mary wondered up and down the streets until a policeman spotted herald took her to Grady Memorial Hospital. The attendants thought that she was a crazy crack head that had gone completely out of her mind. She was scared out of her mind and jumpy as a mouse! Whenever she heard rattling papers, doors creeping opened, these things set off into a frenzied nervous wreck! She had been giving three sedatives of which had no affect of calming her fractured nerves! When the doctor came into the examination area, she leaped under the table and screeched like a frightened kitten! The doctor was a kind gentle physician. He sat on the floor and talked to her as she sat underneath the table. She told him about the violent fight she had with Daren, how he had slammed her up against the walls and onto the floor! Then held a knife to her throat and dared her not to move an inch or he would slash her throat from ear to ear! Daren knew she was a scared naive little country girl who knew nothing about big city life in Atlanta! That's why he savagely attacked her and threatened her with the most powerful organization in the world, The MAFIA!

At that very moment, Mary didn't know how to separate fantasy from the real world! The Doctor reassured her that everything was going to be ok and that he was going to place a security officer at the door to keep her under guarded protection over night.

The moment Daren woke up, he hither streets like a bloodhound tracking its prey. His nose seemed to have had the keened sense of a Mandingo warrior sniffing out her feminine scent in the air. He arrived at the Hospital at 2.30 in the morning and started asking questions? He demanded to be allowed to see Mary and for her to be released into his custody! One of the Nurses told her that she heard Daren asking people in the lobby if they had seen me or knew which room she was in? Frantically she grabbed her clothes and started to climb out the window! The nurse grabbed her legs and pulled her back inside! Mary rolled over on to the floor and screamed, "he is going to killed me! Please help me! I don't want to die! The nurse cradled Mary into her arms and reassured her that she would be safe.

Mary's family was notified to come to the hospital and take her home. They were told that she had been brutally beaten by Daren and was on the verge of having a nervous breakdown! They further advised that She needed to see a psychiatrist for treatment for mental issues!

Her older sister Mahalia and brotherly William brought her back home! Not being aware of the gravity and severity of that brutal and hellish assault that she had received from Daren's violent episodes! They thought she was crazy and were afraid that she might harm herself! Mahalia thought that Mary was going to jump out of the car or grab the stirring wheel! Mary yelled out loudly that she was not crazy but afraid that Daren or the Mafia was going to kill her! She fell back into the seat and buried her face into her hands while sobbing uncontrollably.

When she arrived back at her mother's house, she was distraught, paranoid and in terrible condition. She was even afraid of the air that blew thru the opened window, or running water in the bathroom sink. If her mother opened the window, she would go into a sheer panic, begging and pleading for her not to let the mob rub her out!

That morning her Mother attempted to wake her for breakfast. Mary thought her mother had turned into Daren and was trying to kidnap her! She screamed in terror and fainted! When her mother brought food to her, she thought the food was poisoned and knocked it out of her hands! It got so bad that her mother threatened to send her off to the crazy farm if she didn't get herself together!

Whenever relatives visited, she would run up to the loft and hide in the dark corners! Her mother would coax her down from the loft after everybody had left and read soothing scriptures from the Bible to calm her down and give her some peace of mind!

One day as her mother was reading 121 psalm, Mary felt the power of Almighty God coming inside of her heart. She put her hands on her chest and it didn't beat out of control anymore. She told her mother that she was going outside and breath in some fresh air. She was so happy that the Lord had set her free from torturing fear that had held her captive for a long time! Tears of Joy ran down her mother's face as she watched her baby girl walk outside in the light of day once again!

This joy was short lived. After giving birth to her first child with Daren, Mary eventually found herself trapped back into Daren's web of violence and destruction!

Captivity, one word with so many meanings. There are captives of the mind where one is afraid to be his or her own true self, or to exercise one's thoughts for fear of rejection. And finally, to be captive of one's own heart with no power to resist fleshly and lustful desires!

"How I long to be free and run in the grass and pick the Lilly of the field. What I feel in my soul is the desire to give love and receive love! However, when love is interrupted by the green eyed monster of Jealousy, pain, hate and suffering follows suit!

In my life there has been times of complete happiness that were followed by intervals of complete disarray and mayhem from the fists of the man that profess his undying love towards me in bed, then beat me until tomorrow becomes a new day! We slept so closely as one body during the night, but at daylight I became his bitch or his whore by name! I became his punching bag and blamed for everything that went wrong in his life!

CHAPTER 11B

CAPTIVE OF MY HEART PART 2

Daren was a selfish and arrogant bastard with no moral values whatsoever! His usual routine was to start running around and cheating on Mary with other women every time she became pregnant with child! He got a kick out of hurling insulting names at her! "You fat ugly, good for nothing slut! Every time I turn around you putting another baby on me! Don't no body else want your ugly ass!".

On many occasion he used the family cargo pick up his other women and ride them all around town while drinking stinking and telling lies! Early one morning while gallivanting around, some crazy man started chasing him because he had been sleeping with his wife! The guy threw a brick and smashed one of the rear windows, then ram the backside of the car so hard that he knocked the back bumper off and busted out the tail light.

Daren managed make it back home and hid the car behind the house. How he got into the house so fast, even surprised him. He told Mary that he had an accident but was not clear on the details. Upset, Mary went outside to check the car's damage. Visibly distraught, she went back inside and stoat the backdoor to catch her breath. Glimpsing through the window, she saw a pair of legs sticking from behind the hedge. Mary yelled, aint' no use of you trying to hide! You might as well bring your home wrecking ass in here woman! Daren overheard the heated exchange between the two women and pulled Mary away from the window. Mary looked over his shoulders and saw another woman and two dudes stooping and hiding in the woods! She yelled again, "I told all y'all she devils and he devil dogs to leave me and my husband alone! Get the hell out of here now".

Daren grabbed her and pulled her to the back bedroom where he started slapping and choking her back against the wall! He whispered in her ear, "You lucky bitch! If you didn't have that baby inside you, I'd kill you dead right now! Don't you ever embarass me in front of my friends again! I'm gonna drop my friends off and when I get back, you better have my supper good hot, ready and waiting for me on the table.

When Daren left the house, Mary laid on the floor in utter despair, uncontrollably sobbing and praying for a way out of her violent and loveless marriage with Daren! If not for the love of her children, Mary would have already put an end to her pain and suffering by committing suicide! Just close her eyes and not look into his mean angry eyes any more would have been a great relief!

Mary declared, "You have never been a husband to me or a good father to our children. The only reason that I am staying here is because of our children. You look at your hands and call yourself a monster after you beat me in the face and leave black and blue marks! You say you'll never hit me again, but, two or three days later you become a wild animal and repeat the same vicious assault over and over again! Daren rolled his eyes and blew steam out of his mouth then walked out slamming the door behind him!

Mary thought to herself, Why can't I leave this cruel evil man and stay away from him for good? My heart jumps into my mouth every time he comes near me! Daren has beaten me so much that I cannot hold my head up and coward down like a scared dog! I wonder if death a better fate than to be trapped into this endless nightmare!

Mary knew it was only a matter of time before Daren would comeback home and start kicking the shit out of her battered and bruised body. Especially after he lost his job and could not buy beer and cigarettes for himself and his no good buddies! He was a constant nag and complainer. Mary you didn't cook the food right, you can't even put up groceries right! Do it my way or get the hell out of my house! I was a prisoner of this deranged madman that took pleasure in his grotesque and volatile episodes!

Fear gripped my soul suspending me into stifling silence of a timeless dimension! The sound of my heart beating suddenly rang profusely in my ears like a warrior drum! Daren could strike a final blow to my head and kill me dead at any moment! God please set me free from this evil monster!

"I dreamed of one day holding my head up and smiling at the passers by as I stroll along the sidewalk free at last to come and go as I please! I would be so happy to stand in front of the mirror and put on some pretty red lipstick and makeup and go to the beauty parlor and paint the town red on a girls night outing!

Every breath of life became so precious as I clanged to a mere thimble of hope to see another day! My world grew darker and dismal with every blow from Daren's fists of fury to my head!

Daren came back into the room yelling, We need money to pay the rent and light billi Aint' no dam food in this house! Listen here bitch! You are a woman and you know how to get what we need! You gonna get your ass up on that stage and strip! No two cent job gonna pay all these bills and feed all these scrump snatchers around here! You will do what I say or else, he demanded.

Mary screamed, I am a mother and haven't learned how to put my conscience to sleep yet! You drag me by the hair and beat me! And now you want me to be your whore! You can't keep hurting me like this! I will not do it! You go strip in a gay bar and help take care of this kids that you helped bring into the world!

Festering soars of poverty added insult to injury for Mary! Backed into a corner, she knew she had to fight or die! Red corals of pain and anger lit up and exploded in her heart! Of all the shit you put me through, this is the lowest and dirtiest thing you could ask of me! You no good low down dog want to turn me out and peddle my flesh like a butcher in a supermarket! Hell to the naw! Why don't you man up and get a dam job? You got two strong arms and legs, use them!

Daren slickly replied, "I know some strippers that sell pussy and give blow jobs! But I would rather you give head and keep my pussy clean for me! I don't want no other dicks stuck up in you but mines! I'll bring you home and make sweet, sweet love to my baby all night long!

Mary was furious and yelled hell no! I won't do it! Not by the hairs of my pussy chin, chin! Not even if you huff and puff and blow on it real good! This is it! Go straight to hell Daren! I have had enough of your bull shit! I'm leaving you and going home to mother! I probably catch hell there too! But, at least I won't spend another moment with you laying next to me! Don't call me! Don't look for me! And don't you ever put your hands on me again!

Enraged, Daren grabbed her by the throat and begin choking the life out of her! He slammed her on the floor and pounded her head left and right with his fists! The two of them danced the waltz of death! In a moment of desperation, Mary grabbed a metal candle holder and off the floor and struck Darer. across his head! He rolled over to his side in attempt to recover! Then Mary got to her feet and hit will again knocking him unconscious! She retrieved some personal belongings and ran out the door!

While on her heroic escape, her mind was filled with many questions about life and the love between a man and a woman! "Am I not a person to grow in love and compassion? Why does this black cloud hover over my heart and render me with blind emotions?

CHAPTER 12

HAVING A BABY

OCTOBER 21, 1976

Having a baby can be a wonderful experience if one is prepared to handle such a tremendous responsibility! I was caught in a stressful condition and unprepared to be a new mother! Adoption and abortion were out of the question!

I was growing as big as a house everyday. The first two months I suffered with morning sickness and upset stomach. I felt tired and heavy and cried at the drop of a hat! The worst thing anyone could do was to stare at my basketball belly and laugh at my shape! None of my clothes fitted anymore so I had to buy maternity clothes and big T-shirts at yard sales and thrift stores.

I wasn't alone in my situation, my sisters Amanda and Isabelle were in the same family way too! All three of us girls had our babies in the same month and the same year and at the same hospital! Mother jokingly teased us saying, "Well I know what all my baby girls were doing nine months ago, mmm huh! Aint' that something! As soon as I run up and down these halls with Amanda, here comes Isabelle and Mary moaning and groaning trying to push my sweet precious grand babies. Well, all you girls better get ready, you bout to pay the price with those long, strong, and hard labor pains!

The proudest moments of my life was when I felt the first kick in my belly from my baby! That kick let me know that he was almost ready to come into the world! I never seemed to get enough food to eat. I was always hungry.

I had a name as I entered through the doors of the prenatal clinic, but coming through the double doors, I became a number. Branded and tagged, I was herded in with all the other refers! Number 29 was called by an angry face that peered out of another door. I was anxious as I squeezed through the corridor. The doctor came inside the examining room and instructed me to climb on to the table. The physician was very cold and sterile. The entire experience to me was similar to that of a mad scientist project with me being the human specimen and being stripped of all self respect and humanity and handled like a piece of meat!

Could you please help me up on this table, it is very high and I don't want to fall, I asked. Reluctantly he placed his arm around my huge frame and heaped me up on top. His hands were cold and smelled of antiseptics as he probed inside my vagina during the fetus development exam.

His eyes bulged out of his heads he raised the covers off my Dolly Pardon Breasts that quivered with every breath that I took. Examining them in a circular motion with fingers, his lab jacket popped opened at the center of his trousers exposing large imprints of his rising penis!

I wanted to stick my head underneath the covers when he requested two of his colleagues to come in for consultations concerning my overlarge breast. They were so big that they looked liked two water melons on my chest. I could see their faces turning red as they touched my 77-ff cups. Needless to say I had a truck load of titles for their eyes to feast on! With the completion of the examination, I was instructed to return to my seat in the waiting room. Then 2 hours later the nurse came in, gave me some pills and informed me of the dos and don'ts of my condition and sent me on my merry way.

Ten days later my water broke! I was having some serious pains and yelled for mother to come and help me! Mother, She yelled, the baby is coming!

Mother dropped everything she was doing and yelled, Oh my God the baby is coming! By the time Marie reached her daughter's side, Mary had almost fainted! Marie quickly placed a cold cloth to Mary's forehead and instructed her to breathe slowly through the towel. Then she and her oldest son Walt drove Mary to the hospital.

Marie comforted her baby girl and reassured her that everything was going to be all right. Upon entering the hospital the nurses scolded Mary for screaming and kicking all over the place! They became agitated and moved me into the far back area of the nurses station and into a musty old room. It reminded of the segregated dentist office back in the day.

Suddenly a deep strong pain went all over my body as the muscles contracted inside my stomach and vagina forcing the baby downward to the birthing canal! The nurses showed up late just like the calvary in the cow boy movies! With one hard push and a very loud scream, my first baby boy was born

I was so happy to have brought a new life into the world. My precious little boy was so soft and cuddly and full of love! I felt like I had become a full grown woman, a giver of life! Each day I held him in my arms, breast fed him and changed his poopie diapers let me know of the great responsibility that I bore on my shoulders. I noticed his nails and skin had turned yellow and called for the nurse. She informed me that the doctors had diagnosed him to have Yellow Juantis and had to be put into an incubator and treated with ultra violet rays! I remember peering through the glass and seeing him in a glow of purple lights. My heart went out to him and my worries were eased knowing that he was getting treatment for his guarded condition!

However the next morning the nurse and doctors came into the room with devastating news! Daren had finally showed up at the hospital and demanded to see his baby. When he was denied visitation, he went to the maternity ward and snatched the child out of the incubator and escaped through one of the emergency doors! I was given sedative to calm my nerves after hearing the disturbing news!

I was outraged and yelling to the top of my lungs asking Where is my baby? Somebody please help me find my baby? Two days later a staff member from Grady Hospital called inquiring about information pertaining to a new born baby brought in by his father. The only information the father had shared was that the infant had received treatment at Spalding County Hospital. He had become nervous and abandoned the child.

Upon notifications of her baby's location, Mary called her mother to come to the hospital to help her get dressed and find someone to take her to Grady Hospital and pick up her baby! The pain I felt all over my body was nothing compared to the aching pain in my heart not knowing where my baby was?

As she and I rode in the local taxi cab to Atlanta, she held my hand and told me to calm down and be strong for little Lance! We hurried to the elevator and maternity ward where the kind nurse placed my baby into my arms! I hugged him tightly and gently kissed his innocent little face!

In the mist of our chaotic love hate relationship, we had two more children! I worked very hard to keep food on the table and pampers on their bottoms! I sold scrap metals, aluminum cans, glass bottles at the salvage company! Many people laughed when they saw me at the dump lugging those heavy batteries! I just laughed along with them to keep from crying!

Whenever the heated arguments between my brother David and me, Mother took us down to her little 2 room hideaway shack down in Locust Grove. It was a cozy little cabin with fireplace in the bedroom. I loved to walk down the dirt road and smell the wet muddy clay dirt in autumn. I could hear the ruffling leaves fallen as the wind blew my hair.

CHAPTER 13A

ENTRAPMENT PART 1

OCTOBER 18, 1978

I feel so all alone! Struggling, striving and taking the bitter with the sweet! That one for all, all for one destiny somehow eludes me, leaving me to be a castaway lost in the battering sea of fear, hate and jealousy!

Where is my sister? Where is my brother? Why are we now strangers at war, not giving a dam if one or the other lives or dies? I pray that my children never imitate their violent father or their deranged aunts and uncles! Raising the sword of death to end the flow of life through their veins by their own hands would be too cruel a fate for my eyes to see!

Dearest mother is the rose of peace that holds everything together, she holds all the pieces of our lives in place just like a pin that keeps the grenade from igniting and exploding! I often hear her praying "In thee oh Lord do I put my trust! Hide not though self from my supplications, lest my enemies would devour me and swallow me up! Come to the aide of your servant Lord! Keep me from the violent and wicked man who has purpose to affliction to me! In the shadow of thy wings I will make my refuge until the calamities leave me!"

How many times have I asked the clouds where is my brother David? When we were young, we laughed in the wind and danced on the rose petals that led to love and hope! So weak and curious was he as he walked the road of adventure! So strong was I as I grasped his hand and pulled him across to safety. Those days of trust and caring are stored in my memory waiting to come alive again! David had been bewitched with so many mixed emotions and multiple personalities which left him in a state of confusion and a male identity crisis. His anger and frustration was very dominant and destructive! He was very neat and tidy with his outward appearance, but inside he felt dirty and nasty!

No matter how much he scrubbed the floors or washed the dishes, or portrayed himself in a feminine way, he was still David, not Dianna as he sometimes called himself! His madness led him to become enraged and violent towards me and my children. If he saw a crumb on the table he would yell at my kids and blamed them. I had had enough of his mean and nasty ways! When he snatched my son up by his arm out of his chair, my motherly instincts kicked in and I lit into him like a mad dog knocking him down on the floor! Then I leaped on top of him as we tumbled over and over on the floor! I yelled at him saying, "Don't you ever put your dam hands on my kids again! I am tired of your bullshit! Leave me and my kids alone!

David's very young when he encountered his first imaginary experiences with one of his playmates. He and his little friend were pretending to be young girls sharing an apartment together. They constructed little playhouse made of old plywood and cardboard boxes. Sneaking inside my sister's Mahalie's bedroom he snatched two of her dresses and shoes, then went to the kitchen and picked up some dishes and utensils, snacks and sodas and ran back to the playhouse.

Curious to know what they were up to, I followed him back to their make believe playhouse. Hiding behind a large bush, I watched them enter their castle. Silently I crept closer up to the window, pulled the curtain back and saw them prancing around in their dresses and setting the table with their stolen treats and calling each other honey child and sweetie pie! I covered my mouth with my hand to keep from laughing my ass off at those two little brats! I never told a soul what I had seen that day! However, David may have spotted me through the window as I ran back to the house, but he nevnu said a word!

I was in the family way and pregnant yet again! I went to bed and woke up the next morning with a house full of mean and angry strangers with tempers that flew sky high! Everyone hated each other to the point of death! I couldn't understand how only a few hours earlier, the family was glad to see me, and now when I needed them the most, they were fighting and carrying on like crazy people! I sure wished father was still here! He would whip all our asses and make us be on our best behavior!

David yelled at Mary saying, "Honey, you better sit down! You can't do nothing with that wide load you are carrying! You big pink elephant, waddle, waddle! He teased. Mary replied, "David, I really don't feel like fighting with you today! Can't you see I am about to have this baby anytime now! But remember, when you laugh at me, you are laughing at Mother too when she carried you in her belly for nine hard long months!

David angrily replied, You stupid bitch! I'll knock that baby out of your belly right now! You big fat stinking whore! You think you are so dam smart! Come on Jump bitch! I wants me some Mary meat! Hit me bitch! I will slang your ass into the outer limits and dare you to come back down!

Mother told David to leave Mary alone! "David I am telling you right now to get away from her! Stop yelling and scaring her, she needs to be as comfortable as possible so that mother nature can take its course! I am tired of you carrying on like a maniac! Get the hell out of here now or I will call the Police and have you thrown out! The whole neighborhood can hear you acting like a fool!

David yelled, "Bitch I hate your guts! Why couldn't I have been a girl? I 'll show you how to be a real woman!" David grabbed Mary's arm and twisted it, causing her to scream in pain and agony! Mother pushed him backwards causing him to release Mary's arm! Then she grabbed a bowl from the table and crowned him good on his head! She told him not to come back inside until he calmed the fuck down!

Marie carried Mary and her other 2 kids to stay at her little shack house for a few days. Her young son little Derrick was out side playing when he noticed a gas scooter bike in the back yard went to check it out. Somehow he managed to remove the gas cap and sniff the gasoline inside the tank. Mary heard him calling her. When he saw her coming he yelled, "Momma I want some Ice Cream!" Then he collapsed on to the ground! Frantically she picked him up and carried him inside the house and filled his mouth with mustard to sober him up! After a few days Mother Marie decided to come back to the big house in McDonough.

David was standing in the doorway when they arrived back home. He was bitter and mad as hell that Mother had taken Mary and the kids away for a few days! He was sipping on a cup of coffee while walking around in his head scarf, footies and house coat. He started in on Mary just as she stepped on to the porch. "Bitch, let me straighten you right now! You aint' shit! I am tired of looking at your ugly face! I wish you were dead and buried too long to talk about! I will snatch you balled just like Kojack!

Mary did not utter a word! She just shook her head in disgust and went to her bedroom! David continued his ranting and raving although the night!

Chapter 13B

ENTRAPMENT PART 3

DECEMBER 16, 1986

As the years passed, David became more violent and aggressive towards his sister Mary and her kids! Once again, David and Mary were embroiled into a horrible fight. Fists of fury were flying all over her body, leaving her with a black eye and a busted lip! When will his jealous tirades come to an end? She and her three boys fled back to mother's shack down in the country. They were all crowded in the small cramped bedroom. There was one bunk bed on the left side of the room and one regular size bed on the right side. A single light hung from the ceiling and there were only two electrical outlets per room. The house had a tin top roof, and the porch was made of wood boards loosely nailed to rotten beams. The shack rested on the coldest spot on the road. Late at night the cold winds howled with a strong force causing the trees to bow to its command!

Mary wanted to stay up to the big house during the cold winter month, but David was on the war path and out of control! She hated to see the rain and snow cover the grass with ice cycles that crunched underneath her feet. She found no dry wood or kindling in the wood box. She found a few logs under the porch, but not enough wood to keep a warm set back fire through the night. So, she gathered some wet logs to add to the dry wood fire.

She found some pine straw and used it for kindling to spark the flames! Before she could pitch it into the fireplace, the straw started to move inside the basket. What the hell was going on? She thought.

Looking closer inside, she saw a small black snake poking its head out from the straw! Quickly, she threw the straw, snake basket and all into the fire place, then doused it with kerosene, lit a match and tossed it in and set everything inside on fire! Then watched that snake burn to a crisp!

After that horrendous ordeal, she began making the beds more warm and cozy. She placed three blankets, comforters and her winter coats on the bed to keep everyone safe and warm through the night. They all slept in their jackets, gloves and hoods too! Blistering winds seeped through the cracks in the walls and floors swallowing up the warm air from the crackling fire. She sang sweet lullabies to her precious babies and reassured them that they would make it through the cold bitter night!

Morning arrived with a bang! She felt like a piece of iceberg lettuce! Their frosty breaths spewed like cigarette smoke every time she said good morning to her babies. She was so afraid for her family! How much longer could they fight to survive the onslaught of the brutal weather. Maybe her brother Walt would help them gather some wood to make it through the rest of the week. He lived across the road in an old farm house! Walt was a real down home country boy! He loved to live the country life! Surely he would show his nephews how to survive in the wilderness!

Lance, Marco, and Derrick were so very happy about the upcoming holiday celebrations! They told me that they all had dreamed that were had move into a brand new home on Christmas Day! Inside of this house was a beautiful tree decorated with silver and gold balls dangling from its limbs and twinkling multi-colored lights that cast green, blue, red shadows on the walls. There were lots of gifts stuffed under neath the tree for everyone! They were pretty colored ribbons and bows and name tags on all the packages! Sneaking into the dinning area, the kids caught a glimpse of most delicious treats! There were all kinds of edible goodies, from chocolate cakes, lemon meringue pies, peppermint sticks, lollipops and mountains of ice cream! This hearty spread was as pretty as a Norman Rockwell Christmas Card!

Too Bad it was only a dream so far removed from our humble and meager surroundings, of a two room shack house sealed with cardboard to shield us from the freezing cold winds at night. My oldest son Lance, all of nine years old wrapped up and went outside to fetch some wood for the fireplace! He found an old axe and wagon out back and hurried into the forest. He was stopped in his tracks by a pretty tree and decided to cut it down and bring it back home with him! Lance and his brothers decorated it with strings of popcorn and paper cut outs. They drew a big Santa Face and nailed it to the door outside! Then the boys picked up the bucket that held the tree and sat it on the porch!

Lance was the first to wake the next morning. He was eager to see if Santa Clause had come and left presents for himself and his brothers! He was stunned to see that his Christmas tree was gone when he looked outside! All that was left of the tree were a string of pop corn and paper cut outs blowing in the wind! He smiled and said, "Its ok! Santa must have come by and picked it up last night!

They had a joyful Christmas after all! Mary pulled out an army bag chucked full of toys she had gotten from the goodwill store and gave them to her kids! They were so surprised and happy to get those toys! The kids had toy soldiers, pop guns, plastic bats, catcher's mitt, and toy cars! Then she got the fire going and cooked some bacon and eggs, grits and grilled toast for breakfast!

Preparing for another turbulent night in their frozen ice castle, she told the boys to join her in prayer at the foot of the bed! They all gathered on their knees and repeated the Lord's Prayer and thanked him for keeping them safe!

After placing 3 big logs on top of the simmering ashes, they all went to bed. Late into the night, Mary awoke to a loud ringing in her ears. It was so loud that it made her get out of bed! She was frightened because she kept hearing this voice telling her to "Get up now!" The kids were asleep and there was no one else in the room! Thinking to herself she said, I may as well check on this fire!

Mary noticed that the carpet was smoldering with coals about to blaze up in flames! She leaped to her feet, grabbed the poker and raked the hot coals back into the fire place! She was so grateful to God for sending his angels to wake her up and save her and her family!

She tried to come back home many times! Ignoring the fact that she did not leave on her own, she was driven away by vial malicious words that left scars and wounds deeply imbedded into her heart! Watching her brothers and sisters taking sheer pleasure in her unfortunate circumstances during crucial times in her life was a bitter pill for her to swallow! Thinking that her kids would be better off without a mother, she contemplated committing suicide to rid herself of all the guilt of not being able to care for her children!

She offered love and was rejected! The long road to survival was falloff thorns that cut deep into her flesh! However modest or unpredictable her life had been, she continued to search for love, joy and happiness! Once the grass is cut, it withers and dies, leaving only its roots that burst through the soil, sprouting a new blade of grass. Mary stretched out her arms reaching to the heavens to feast on the love of her heavenly father, Almighty God!

CHAPTER 14

MY MOMMA ANNA

Whenever I am so lost and need a friend indeed, I often think of my other mother, a stranger I came to know as My Momma Anna! Though had never met in life before, being the motherly figure that she was, without any hesitation, she gathered me and all my kids up and brought us home to live with her and her family!

Life at home with David was unbearable! He never let up the pressure! He constantly badgered Mary with jealous tirades! His words were so painful that they caused deep mental torture to Mary and her kids! David anger and violent outbursts were uncontrollable and very dangerous! He attacked her in front of her new boyfriend! He was mad because her new friend bought her a chicken snack from Big Chic Restaurant. And also bought her kids some snacks and candies from the Nite Owl store.

He was like a wild beast! Taring at her clothes until her bare chest bled from his sharp tiger claws! David was a bully and alcoholic who hated women with a passion! Mother didn't know what to do? She had sympathy for David because he was sick in the head! His problems could have easily been resolved with good old fashion ass whooping with a rapid motion licking stick! If only your father was here, he would knock some sense into your head, she angrily said!

David knew would get on mother's nerves by parading about the house in full drag, just acting like a fool! He would twist across the flooring a flirty strut, batting his eyes, changing his voice prancing around as he pretended to do household chores.

David, she called. I have had enough of your mess now! You are going to calm down and leave your sister alone! She has already been beaten and tortured by her crazy baby daddy! Give me and her a break, Dammit!

David's bulging eyes turned red with fire as he hurled himself into Mary's trembling body, unleashing a barrage of punches, kicks, slaps across the face before choking her down to the floor with his big long fingers! Mother pushed David to the floor to loose his deadly grip from Mary's neck!

It was time for Mary to leave her mother's home. She had a few dollars left in her pocket for gas but not enough to pay for a hotel. Her old station wagon was the only roof she had to call her own! She made some curtains on strings to cover the back windows of her car. Then she loaded some can goods and dry goods, snacks and warm blankets inside her car. She didn't know where she and her kids were going but she was getting the hell away from David ASAP!

She ended up parking her car on a side road that stretched along beside the railroad tracks! She and her kids were like a band of gypsies living in the wilderness! Every morning she drove to the nearest service station to use the bathroom and wash up in the sink. Sometimes she borrowed toilet paper too to wipe snotty noses.

I remember the day I met Big Momma Anna. The kids and I were heading back to our make shift hobo camp, when I noticed this large big bone woman walking down the street. Following closely behind her were a long string of kids that could fill my station wagon to the brim! This woman looked like she could not go any further on her journey. I pulled up beside her and ask if she needed help? She said that she and her kids needed a ride to the clinic for check up and a ride back home! I agreed to take her and her family to the clinic and back home. I ask her if she knew of any cheap houses for rent in town? She said no but she would let me know if something comes up.

Big Momma Anna knew instantly that I had been sleeping in my car! She boldly told me that she knew I and my kids were sleeping in my car. Then she offered to let me and my kids come live with her and her family. I didn't know what to think of this strange woman offering to share her home with me and my kids? I could tell that she too had faced some hard challenges in her life!

Momma Anna was blunt when she said that she did not live in a shiny palace, but, I was welcomed to stay with her and her family as long as I wanted! "I have no running water or toilet, my furniture is old, everything is comfortable and lived in! My doors are opened and you are welcomed to come on in and take a load off girl! We are home!" Let me show you exactly what I mean, she jokingly said.

My eyes could not believe what they were seeing! Inside her house looked liked the hull of Noah's Ark and had a foul stinking odor that floated upward and hit me in the face as I walk through the door! There were baby chicks flapping their tiny wings and chirping at my feet! Chicken feed and poop all over the floor! She had 2 kittens and 2 pups and one duck too! She and her kids seem perfectly happy wallowing in filth with all these animals!

This woman was so very kind and loving, with a heart of gold! She was the queen mother and ruler over her dirty palace! What you saw is what you got! She asked no questions and made no boundaries and treated us like her own flesh and blood! What she ate, we ate, where she went, we went! Some days were lean without any food, but she always came up with some rare entree' once eaten by her ancestors to fill all our hungry bellies.

At least we were safe and no longer sitting by the railroad tracks, looking up at the stars and too afraid to close our eyes at night. In the afternoon we would go into the woods and hunt for pretty sweet smelling Dog Wood Trees. They blossomed in many pastel colors. And sometimes the kids would find patches of wild strawberries, black berries, plumbs, apples and pear trees. Filled with excitement and the spirit of adventure, we forged onward into the untamed forest, oblivious to the imminent dangers of creepy crawlers and slithering snakes with deadly kisses lurking underneath the withered leaves and fallen branches on the ground! The kids even found a sparkling pond to cool their hot feet while splashing and playing in the water! The plants and flowers shimmered with life! I could feel them breathing as the wind whispered to the rustling leaves! I named this hidden garden The Creature. This pond became our water supply!

Every morning, Momma Anna would gather the dirty laundry and put the clothes in a wash tub to soak before washing them. Through the good times and the bad times as long as we were together, we enjoyed the simple country life!

She made a fishing rod out of strings and branches to catch some brims for supper! In order to get to the pond, we had to cross fields of growing soy beans and water melons. Placing little Derrick on my shoulders, I waded through the thick vines and bushes! I could tell we were getting close when the large mosquitos attacked us in droves! We caught mostly fresh water brims, a few cat fish. And Big Momma caught an old snappy turtle. Smacking her lips and rubbing her big belly, she said that turtle meat was better than brims anyway of the week! I got sick watching those frog legs jumping in the hot grease! I guessed I must have lost about twenty pounds during my stay with her and her family. Everyone wondered how I got so slim? I missed a lot of meals, making sure that my boys would have full bellies went to bed! Every Tuesday was wood fetching day. Big Momma Anna swung her axe like a man, chopping logs to keep all of us warm through the cold winter nights. The boys and I gathered all the kindling and straw to help get the fire started.

I ran into mother while in town one day. She seemed pleased to see me and the voys! "Now Mary, you know you can come back home! You have just as much right to live there as David! I won't let him hurt you and the kids again! Please come home now! The neighbors have been asking questions about you! Ms Patty Lee told me she saw you in Madison's grocery store and you looked like you had been on a starvation diet!"

Returning to Big Momma Anna's house, I found her stripping another small limb to make a fishing pole. She wanted to go fishing again. She and I strolled through the woods to the pond and set down on the muddy banks. The pond was so clear that I could see pretty rocks and fishes at the bottom as water flowed down stream.

Momma Anna sat down and filled her jaw with some chewing tobacco. Then she said, well if you are thinking about going back home, I wanna let you know I will miss you and the kids! I think of you like you are my own daughter and you are very dear to my heart! I am gonna miss you and the boys! You take care of my babies and take care of you too daughter! Please come back and visit with me sometimes!

We hugged each other in a warm and loving embrace as showers of tears rolled down our cheeks! Good bye dear sweet Momma Anna! I shall miss you too! I will never forget the kindness and love you showed to me and my kids! You will always have a place in my heart!

CHAPTER 15

THE OTHER MAN

L iving in a fantasy world became detrimental to Mary's sanity! She was consumed in a dream world that became more real to her mind than reality itself! When confronted with logic and reasoning, she sometimes chose to walk on the thin line of neutrality! In her real world, it was painful to live with a man that did not love or respect her! She was trapped with their children and had no way out of a bad situation! She was shoved out of a playground and landed into a life of bondage and servitude with a mad raving monster!

All of his vicious assaults erased any love that she had ever felt for this man! Life with Daron was almost unbearable! She was battered and beaten night and day! Sleep was the only freedom she knew to rid herself of this living hell! At least in her dreams she could fall into the arms of a loving and caring man that would cherish every kiss that their lips tasted and drank from the goblet of passion!

In the safety and seclusion of her bedroom, Mary began to drift into a strange and haunting dream! She was falling down a long shadowy tunnel when suddenly she landed in front of a local Night Club. The music was loud as it blasted through the door. With all the crazy shit that had invaded her day, it sure would be nice to sip on a refreshing glass of Margarita with salted rim, she thought.

Mary was decked out in sparkling attire! She was looking good and smelling good and ready for some action! The lights were flashing bright colors on the mirrors that covered the surrounding walls. They were enticing her to get out there and shake her ass on the dance floor!

All eyes were on Mary as she started swinging and swaying her body in a sultry dance!

Looking across the room Mary saw a very handsome face glaring at her every motion. He was as dark as the night with strong sexy features! She long to get closer to him and feel his hot breath teasing the back of her neck as he stills a soft sweet kiss! His eyes set her heart to flames! What kind of power could this man have to excite her emotions without ever touching her hungry body!

Its seemed as though time was standing still! What a beautiful and magnificent place to be, in a splendorous moment frozen in time from a wonderful new Dimension of her mind! Where was this place and who was the owner of such a fine establishment? She thought.

The ladies wore beautiful dresses, exquisite jewelry, and lavish furs! The men were dressed to the nines as well with their elegant suits and their gold pocket watches with pretty gold chains! The handsome man she saw earlier came and stood by her side, held out his hand and ask her to join him on the dance floor?

Mary reluctantly accepted his request. Then she asked, what is your name and where is the place located? He proudly answered, my name is Philip. And you are where you belong, here in my arms! Mary replied, "What the hell do you mean? Who the hell are You? Philip replied, Oh my darling wife, I am so happy that you have come back to me! I have waited for so long to tell you that I love you forever! Grasping for air, Mary said, "You are crazy! Don't come near me! Help me somebody Please help me!"

Philip grabbed Mary's arm and pulled her closer to his chest as she tried to leave the dance floor! He softly whispered in her ear, "You are my beloved forever and always! I will never let you go

Fleeing from his embrace, Mary stumbled upon a stairway of silver and gold! At the top the stairway of pure shiny silver! Mary looked back and saw Philip running fast behind her! Turning the knob, she ran frantically into the dark room. She could hear Philip's foot steps as he came inside and turn on the light switch! Everything in the room looked as though it had not been disturbed for a long time! There was a pretty silver handled comb and brush set resting on the vanity along with fancy perfume spray bottles. On the wall over the mantle was a portrait of Philip and his beautiful wife! Mary was shocked to see the uncanny resemblance she shared with this woman! It was just like looking at her reflection in the mirror.

Mary picked up a bottle of perfume and inhaled it's intoxicating scent! It was called FOREVER YOURS! The perfume made her fill faint and unsteady as she leaned into the wall in a panic! Everything started spinning as she saw herself gravely ill and laying in bed! Philip explained that his wife had died of pneumonia, leaving him alone and empty!

Mary envied this woman so very much because she was so cherished and loved by her husband! She would have given a treasure if Daron loved her half as much!

Mary could not help staring at the picture on the wall. She stood motionless like a statue in the center of a museum as he opened the door! Love perfumed the air with irresistible desire! Slowly approaching her, his eyes held her captive in a sedated trans! Hot burning coils engulfed her body into a towering inferno as his quivering lips pressed tenderly against her cheeks! The haunting aroma of love hurled her into the galaxy of rapture! Its sweet fragrance appeased her senses as it rocked and cradled her into hot blazing passion and caused her to lose all restraints and succumb to an exquisite moment of pleasure and desire!

Mary surrendered to Philip's sensual advances and allowed him to shower her with his love! Her lips trembled and she melted like butter into his big strong arms! How sweet his lips tasted as he gave her a tongue lashing all over her body, from head to toe! He seemed so strong and masterful and yet so gentle as he laid her onto the bed while whispering in her ear, "I want you ! I need you! You are a rhapsody to my heart! The melody of vivacious beauty captures my soul and renders me to be your slave! I am like a hungry baby suckling to your sweet nipples until I am full of your sweet nectar!! I must tell you that you are my soul and spirit, you take away all the pain deep in my mind and fill me with infinite joy! Please tell me that you are mine forever!

Mary replied, "That I would be allowed one possession, to be with you forever would be so utterly delectable! Every morning I wake up and stare into your wicked delicious eyes and know that you are all the man I need, and all the man I want! You! You! You! Mean the world to me! Come! Let us make hot burning love between these sheet, that we shall never forget!"

The moment he touched her hand and led her into his world, She was captivated! Everything was so beautiful in its layered angelic form! Yet Mary felt out of place like a cherished keepsake trinket on his grand mantle! Being with Philip made her feel whole but deep inside her soul, she knew she could not live in an imaginary world! No matter how much Philip professed his love for her, She knew that he was in love with a lingering memory of his beloved wife!

Mary was forced to the realization that she had to wake up and come back to her own reality even as dismal as it might have been! She had to get back to her children whom she loved with all her being! Before waking up from this beautiful dream, she took one last look at Philip and his monumental shrine to his beloved wife as it glisten into her eyes!

She could hear the clock chiming and ticking louder and louder as she woke up! She could smell the sweet fragrance of roses as she staggered from the bed to the bathroom in a daze! She looked down on the bathroom sink and saw a beautiful red rose in the center of a love poem she had written days earlier!

A LOVER'S DREAM

Love slipped through my fingers like running water streaming down a noisy brook. Its strength clashed my heart with the force of tidal wave, sweeping me into a turbulent storm at sea! My emotions tumbled the deep black waters of heartbreak hotel! My eyes fed themselves on dwindling declaration of undying love as we gaily toasted to love one another forever and forever!

I long for the magic touch that ignite the passion in my soul, releasing emotions that soar to towering heights, as I reach total ecstasy! I want to feel your hot blood next to my skin, bathe in the rapture of hot wild fires and feel flaming torch of desire burning inside me!

Paint me with exotic lights fashioned after Venus and Athena! For you are my pilot in flight of a unforgettable infinite pleasure!

Shall I be a castaway drifting in an endless sea, lost from my love forever? Grant me that one precious wish that I may dance in the rain of contentment and blossom into a rejuvenated flower of desire! Please let the reign of sizzling passion spread like a contagious fever, and cover my entire mind, body and soul with everlasting joy!

CHAPTER 16

THE TROPHY

Mary was walking to the store one day with all her kids strolling along beside her, when she happened to run into two free spirited and opinionated young girls, Mary Anne and Betty Boo. The party girls as they were sometimes called, loved to enjoy life to its fullest potential. Whenever they showed up at a party, everybody knew they were going to have a funky good time!

Needless to say, they corrupted Mary with their wonderful jest for life! Mary Anne noticed Mary boyish look and said, "Girl its time for you to take off that man shirt and hood and start looking like the pretty girl that you are! Hold your head up and walk proud! You are not the only girl in the world to have kids these days! We heard your mean crazy brother yelling and screaming at you and your kids all the way down the street!

Sonya's Playpen, a local night spot was having their annual Miss Sony's Pageant. Mary Anne had entered the competition and asked her to enter the contest too! Mary said that she had to take care of her kids and didn't have time to be in a pageant. Mary wanted desperately to change her looks and start wearing lip stick and heels again! She thought long and hard before calling Mary Anne and give her the good news that she had decided to enter the pageant contest. That is of course if she and her friend Betty Boo would help her get ready for this event!

Mary Anne and Betty Boo became her mentors. They helped her prepare for the big event by styling her pretty long brown hair, doing her make up and lending her some outfits from their closets. The girls taught her how to sashay down the run way and do the pageant wave! Then they demonstrated to her how to pose and perform some hot new dance steps too! Betty Boo brought over some garment selection for Mary to try on as well! Both the girls would stand back, put their hands underneath their chin and say, "Hmmmm! That works for me! Oh you look fabulous! Simply gorgeous! Girl friend!

Mary was still a bit uneasy about being in the contest! Her mind flashed back to the insults and betrayals from her best friends from her high school days! Those awful memories still lingered in the back of her mind! She argued inwardly in her mind saying, Mary Anne and Betty Boo had become her newest best friends and she was not going to let old painful memories get in the way! It was time for her to come out of her shell and show the world know who she was!

Mary decided to talk to her mother Marie before jumping in feet first into a beauty pageant arena that she knew little about. Her Mother said, "The choice is up to you Mary! But I wanna caution you about some people who don't like light skinned folk like us! What if crazy Daren shows up and drag you off the stage? You just be careful if you decide to go ahead with your plans!

David was listening to their conversations as he pretended to sweep the hallway. He jokingly replied, "You know you wouldn't even win fifth place! You fat ugly hog! Oink! Oink! You better stay home with your crumb snatching brats, nobody wanna look at you wide load anyway!

Mary quickly replied, "Only Faggots are drag Queens honey! You just wish you were a real woman! Nobody wants to look at you with your ugly face on! Begone devil from the pits of hell!" David stumbled and fell to the floor as he took a swing at Mary with the broom! She giggled as she ran quickly passed him! She hurried to Mary Anne House to Prepare for the pageant.

For the evening wear competition, she wore a beautiful white French dress and jacket with feather trim! Accessories were white gloves and pumps and matching feather earrings. For dressy Casual scene, she wore a gold and black gypsy jumpsuit with matching gold hair combs and dangling gold earrings. Mary strutted down the runway doing a sensual gypsy rumba dance. For the Sport scene, she wore a hot sexy red leather pant suit, red boots and matching red Bat Man Shades.

Mary arrived at the club in a Carol Burnett costume. She had a grandma scarf wrapped around her head, a long green dress, a Burgundy coat and red with white tennis shoes! Everyone laughed as she hurried to the dressing room to make a total transformation. She laughed right along with them, knowing the audience was in for a big surprise!

The other contestants were so sure of themselves when she first entered the room, but suddenly their eyes started twitching and their nerves crawled up their backs as they watched her unbelievable transformation! The other girls rolled their eyes while elbowing each other in their sides! One of the girls was so jealous that she jumped front of me in the mirror and made an ugly face!

Mary was so excited as the announcer called her name! "Miss Mary Lawrence! Mary resides in McDonough Ga. Her hobbies are singing, dancing, writing short stories and poems! How lovely you look tonight!

Standing their with all the other contestants, She was nervous as a cat, yet she wore a lovely smile that exuded confidence!

The announcer finally came back with the decision from the five panel judges seated at the table!" Ladies and Gentlemen! After careful and long deliberations, we have the decisions from our distinguished judges! Our Third Place winner is contestant number 3, Miss Patricia Sims from Jackson GA! The audience applauded as she stepped out in front and received her trophy!

Mary spotted David's angry face glaring at her as she glanced out into the audience! Oh no, she thought!"I can't lose now! Please God have mercy on me! A Second Place winner was called. Ms Starsha Vierra, from Atlanta Ga is our Second Place winner!

Our First Place Winner is Cookie Rynolds from Stockbridge Ga! The audience saluted her as she was presented with her trophy for First Place!

And now Ladies and Gentlemen! It is time to call our winner for the Title and Crown of Miss Sonya's Playpen ! This is a stunning and magnificent conclusion for everyone tonight! And now, The winner for the Coveted Title and Crown of Miss Sonya Playpen is a local resident! She is a talented writer and songstress! And the winner is Miss Mary Lawrence!

Mary froze in utter shock as the announcer called her name for a second time! The audience went wild with thunderous applause! Betty Boo waved and pointed at Mary, telling her to go and claim her Crown! The lights overhead flickered in her eyes like flaming candles with golden hues! Mary felt like a Queen as she waved to everyone! Cameras flashed to capture that priceless moment!

David got so mad when he saw his sister Mary's picture holding her big Gigantic Trophy and wearing her Beautiful Crown in the Henry Neighbors News Paper the next day! He was determined to destroy her happy celebration and accomplishment and left no stone unturned to have his revenge.

Every day He plotted and schemed to make her life a living hell! He was ate up inside with so much hate and distain for his sister!

Maybe one day his cold black heart would come to love and cherish his big sister and adoring nephews! One can only hope and pray for a miracle! But for now Mary could only dream on and dream on!!

CHAPTER 17

FROM BOY TO MAN

B ored at watching the chickens run back and forth across the yard, Mary called her friend Sheila to see what she was up to? Sheila said that she was gonna hang out at The Country Club, play some spade and watch the dance contest! The club was a located in a big old building with lots of space. The walls were covered with flashing neon lights and mirrors.

Sheila was an old school chum from way back in the day. She was a party girl, known for wearing kooky outfits from fairy tales and old classic movies and cartoon characters! Laying out her clothing on the bed, we went down the line of elimination! Too short, too long, too big and too ugly! I called out for the magic scissors and commanded, " Inspire me!" One, two and three cuts and I had made the sexiest dress that my eyes had ever seen! I had a slanted bottom to show off my Tina Turner Le shapely body. Another cut left a sexy bare shoulder! Sheila cut off her sleeves to make a belt! Then cut a V in the front of her dress to show off her sexy breasts! Then we gave each other a head to toe review and finger snap approval!

Driving to the club, Sheila kept asking, "Do I look all right? Girl you look simply marvelous! I replied. Sheila was an untamed wild cat and seductress! She loved to tease the weak minded guys and nerds! She always wanted to look the best, be the best, and get all the attention!

It seemed as though I was given a second chance relive those teenage years that were tragically stollen from me! I still felt like a sweet sixteen year old girl going her first prom! Arriving at the club, we had the attention of every man and woman in the place! We strolled pass the bar and headed for rest room! We were so delighted to have all eyes glued to our every motion!

While sitting at the bar, a tall handsome man came over and offered to buy us drinks. Sheila commented that he seemed to be staggering a bit! "Lets have a little fun with him, she joked. He was a bit awkward, like a clumsy ten year old trapped in a man's body! "Well, ok, but don't you go too far Sheila! Let the games begin! I replied.

Further observation revealed this tall handsome strap of a man to be a shy little boy crying out for someone to free him from his ignorance of manhood! All this fineness and yet he was a virgin! I knew Sheila was plotting and scheming to wrap him around her little finger, shaking loose all the coins from his pocket, then, dropping him like a piece of trash! She winked her eyes and signaled for me to keep him occupied until she returned from the bar with some strong alcoholic beverages! In her absence I told him to get lost ore he would wish he never seen or spoken to us!

Mary comely said, " Listen here friend, I'm not trying to be funny but, you need to shove off and get lost! You flirting around like a fly bout to caught in a Webb of trouble! You better get gone before you are swallowed up by the evil widow spider! Please find you another toy to play with! Alex stupidly replied, "Maybe I want to get eaten alive! Besides, I am not interested in your friend. I am interested in you! Mary replied, " Forget about it! Not in this lifetime sugar! Alex heartily replied, You got a good heart. Hey can I catch a ride home?

Sheila was furious when she found out that Mary was trying to steer Alex away from her evil clutches! Mary ushered Alex toward the exit doors where they hastily rushed out to the parking lot and jumped inside her car!

Alex explained that he had lived with strict parents who had not allowed him to court or date any girls. His father had an awful mean streak and was jealous of his own son! He was a violent control freak who beat his wife and son into obedient slaves! One day he put Alex out in the streets on a cold night for talking to his own mother!

The evil tyrant took Alex out of school and forced him into working some obscure job on their land lord's farm. Then late at night after Alex was resting from working all day, his father would crawl to the bed where he was asleep and steal his meager 16 dollar wages!

Finally Alex ran away from home at the tender age of 14 and started living on his employers farm! At 18 years old, He did not have a car but was desperate to go out to a local night club! He peddled five miles on his bicycle to the club that night! Alex was determined to find a new friend! He had grown tired of the loneliness and emptiness of his shallow world and was willing to go through extreme measures to find a new friend and perhaps somebody to love. He told Mary how he sat in his room for hours daydreaming of sharing his bed with a loving and caring lady friend! He also confided to Mary that he was a virgin!

When the two of them arrived at Alex's home, He pleaded for her to come inside and talk for a while! Pacing up and down the floor he blurted out and ask Mary to make hot Passionate love to him! He wanted to feel her hot breath flowing all over his hungry body! Mary could feel him shaking all over as she pulled him closer to her panting breasts! Slowly she unbuttoned and slipped him out of his shirt. Then teasingly unzipped and dropped his trousers to the floor! Shoving her tongue deep inside his mouth, tasting his tonsils while rubbing on his ass with her intrusive fingers! Her eyes lit up with delight as she gazed upon his muscular frame! Alex had all the tools of pleasure any woman could ever desire, but, he did not know what the hell to do with them! Grabbing his big hard cock, she skinned it back to show its juicy pink mouth! Alex began to moan with every stroke of her hand jacking his dick off and fell back onto the sofa in a breathless surrender! Falling onto her knees in front of him, she lowered her head and begin licking and kissing his dick! Then suddenly she shoved his dick deep in and out of her mouth with rapid motion! Sucking and pleasuring him until hot juicy cum erupted from his throwing tool!

Quickly, she sat on top of his body and placed his penis into her quivering pussy and began furiously riding it so hard and strong until his dick exploded with hot juicy nectars as she squeezed him tightly and felt him oozing inside of her body!

Exhausted, she fell to the floor with her legs wide opened, exposing her hot sweet pussy! Alex was so very grateful to her for sharing her bare naked ass with him! He was like a sweet gentle little puppy, eager to please her as well! Lying beside her he started kissing the back of her neck while fondling her breast with his big hands, then kissing her nipples with his hungry lips! He was so eager to feast on the sweet nectar inside her pussy walls! Mary began to moan as he lowered his face and stuck his luscious tongue deep inside her vagina! She wanted to feel his tongue and his penis inside her pussy at the same time!

Alex stuck his long finger up the canals of her ass while continuing to suck and lick on her clitoris and driving her wild as she meowed and purred like a wild cat! Sensing that she was about to reach her climax, he pulled himself back up to her tits, shoved them into his mouth and lunged his big throbbing rod inside of her pussy again, fusing more flames of heaping fire all over her shivering body! He was sucking her tits and pumping that good dick deep inside of her with rapid motion until they both exploded into a chunk of burning desire at the same time! Wow What a wonderful feeling of passion they shared together!

Alex and Mary became great friends! She always remembered him with great love and devotion! It was sheer delight for her watching him grow into the man that he wanted to be! Helping him crossed the naive barriers that had plagued his world, and setting him free from the memories of his father beating him and not allowing him to go to school was a great accomplishment for these two unlikely lovers! Mary also carried Alex to visit with his dear precious beloved mother!

Mary watched from her car as Alex's mother greeted her son with opened arms! The reunion was so beautiful as they laughed and cried while holding each other so close! It was now time for Mary to make her grand exit! Alex was happy safe in the arms of his dear sweet mother! At last, he had become a wonderful and great man!

CHAPTER 18

SEDUCTION THE LOVE GAME

B eing notified of my son's six year birthday coming soon, I was sent a memoranda from my case worker at DEFACS that I should start looking for work, get pregnant or enroll in some type of vocational training to continue receiving benefits. The rule was that when the youngest child turned six years old, the mother is no longer eligible to remain on the AFDC PROGRAM as a homemaker. She either had to sign up for their welfare to work program, find a job on her own, have another baby, or enroll in some vocational school. I was told that the only opening through their program at the time was a household domestic worker. I would have to clean up the individual's home, cook meals, do the laundry and assist with personal grooming without any extra pay other than the small AFDC check. This seemed so unfair to perform all those duties and not get paid one red cent extra! I sure as hell didn't want to have another baby just to take the heat off of my situation!

I met the deadline and was enrolled in a vocational training center. Classes were brief, with hardly any time to comprehend the lessons. My case worker seemed disappointed that I chose to further my education. I guess she wanted me to clean her house for slave wages!

I starting my studies at Ashford School of Technology. It was there that I met a smooth and slick talking professor. He words were so proper and his attire was immaculate! What I thought was intelligence behind those somber eyes was a wicked wizard of sexual perversions! He was a pain freak who took pleasure in bondage love games! He viewed me as a country little dwarf desperate to please him in every form and fashion of his sick demented games! He was a dark overlord waiting to crush my wings!

I longed to be in the classroom beside him as he strolled past my desk wearing those sexy glasses while holding pin and papers in tow, eager to mark failing grade to anyone that tested his power of authority! My eyes lit up like twinkling stars whenever he glanced in my direction, flashing that sexy smile and clutching his chin with his hand! He was arrogant and very manipulating to such a backwoods country bumpkin like myself! Yes, I loved to be the apple for the teacher! Bite me baby!

Do my eyes deceive me with this heavenly vision of this fine good looking hunk of a man! He was tall and slender in stature, with a stern serious look on his face! Professor Morningham carried an air of distinction and sophistication proudly upon his shoulders! He had a way of clearing his throat that sent goose bumps all up and down my spine! I loved every moment being in his class as he called my name to answer questions about week end reading assignments.

I began day dreaming, pondering in my mind, going out on a date with such a handsome and intelligent man as him! I could feel his long fingers dancing up and down my spine as he wrote the lesson of the day on the black board.

At one point, however, I thought he was just a flirt. Especially when all the female classmates swooned all over him, and he seemed to enjoy getting all the attention!

Everyday the heat got hotter! I thought of accidentally bumping into him and starting up a conversation outside of the classroom. Finally my wish had come true! The professor cornered me outside of the Teacher's lounge, gave me his number and invited me to call if I needed help with my studies! Well, well, well! I was knocked off my feet! I felt like the best little girl scout who had sold the most cookies and won the big prize! I remember talking inwardly to myself and saying, "Come on now Mary, you know he wouldn't fathom in his wildest dreams of being in a real relationship with you! And why not I asked? Anyway, he did give me his number!"

Each dial tone of his phone number brought me closer to the man I longed to holding my arms! I was pleased to know that he had been thinking about me too! I was nervous when he answered his phone!

Professor cheerfully answered saying, " Well hello there! I have been waiting for your call! I noticed you in my class and wondered why you always stared so intensely at everything? Have we ever met before? You are a very interesting young lady and I sure would like to get to know you a little better!

I was acting all shy and reluctant, not knowing what to say to his dinner invitation! I made some flimsy excuse and ask to take a rain check for a later date. Why was I running like scared little rabbit in a cabbage patch, dodging a loaded gun!

Just thinking about our earlier conversation sent my head in a tail spin just filled with wicked delicious and insatiable thoughts! I gave him a second call the next day and accepted his invitation for dinner! He said that he had a special place he wanted to show me! Just maybe his plans were to show me his private palace of romantic interludes!

Gazing into his big mysterious eyes, I felt the roaring thunder and lightening ignite the flames of desire inside of my quivering heart! Its deep emotion lashed through my hot burning flesh like a blazing inferno! I loved the feel of his sumptuous lips gently kissing my cheeks! With his big strong arm he swept me off my feet and up into his tender embrace! Then laid me onto his bed like I was a rare diamond!

I could feel his long hard cock rubbing against the center my hot wet pussy as himself all over me while whispering sweet notions into my ears!

I tried to resist his sexual advances but my emotions melted like butter as I surrendered to his sweet love and affection! I was his flavorful stick of peppermint candy that he wanted to unwrap and devour with his hungry lips from head to toe!

His words sere soft and juicy like luscious delicious pineapple! Hastely unbuttoning his belt and unzipping his trousers, he pulled out his long sword of pleasure and placed it into my trembling hand! The naughty professor began nibbling at my breast like a hungry baby! I felt electricity serge although me as he pushed his long tool inside my velvet pussy walls! The heat rose high from our two imploding bodies united in uncontrollable passion! It was as though I had known this man for all eternity! The naughty professor slowly worked his sharp tongue down to my fury garden where he harvested my juicy sweet nectar! He licked my pussy walls until I blossomed into a rejuvenated flower of desire!

Our bodies simultaneously erupted with hot oozing silvery white cum like a volcano!

Two weeks later, Professor Morningham informed me that he was going to Indiana to visit his family. So afraid that he would forget all about me, I wrote him a love poem and slipped it into his coat pocket. Surely as the days passed, he would have occasion to read it from time to time, I hoped!

CHAPTER 19

TASTING HOLLYWOOD

The night was colored brightly with twinkling stars! Vehicles sped down the streets like they were connected to carousel bobbing up and down on the poles and getting no where fast! It seemed as though the sky was opening up its vast images to me!

My cousin Audra and I had just visited a disco off Cambelton Street. And let me tell you, the floor was packed full with guys and gals twisting and turning their bodies like snakes while dancing to the techno melody! We were all in the party mood, trying to find any kind of escape to life's everyday challenges! After hours of flirting with those fine good looking brothers, we called it a night and stopped at a burger joint on the way home!

I felt a cold chill as I walked through the doors of the restaurant. Audra spotted a guy in the far corner across from the counter. He looked as if he was trying to hide from someone! She barged over and sat down next to him! I guessed she found her a date for the night. As I proceeded to the counter and placed my order for hash browns, scattered covered and smothered, I caught the glimpse of a handsome stranger's eye! Hmmm! He must be sizing me up, huh! Finally he came over to where I was standing and introduce himself to me as Moses! What an odd name I replied. Flashing his business card, his arrogant nature soared to towering heights! I was very impressed with his conversation and also his sexy rugged appearance!

He said that he was a manager and music producer visiting from Atlanta in search of new talent. Wow, I thought I had hit the jack pot! I had better grab this golden opportunity and hold on tight! I was a very naive young girl with big dreams! I knew that if I didn't pursue this

111

chance encounter with destiny, I would always wonder how it would have turned out! I wanted to be a super star and I was willing to do whatever it took to get to that spotlight!

He asked me to accompany him to his home where we could have a more private conversation and get down to business! His name sounded so biblical and spiritual! But I didn't know if his heart was pure and full of love or black as the night and pure evil! Hesitantly I accepted his invitation to join him at his apartment and get to know him a little better!

I prayed inwardly that he was not a drug addict or sex freak? Moses was so attentive and careful not to show his true dark side! He said that he was the biggest promoter and agent in the south and that he was gonna put me up in the bright lights and make me a super star!

Arriving at his place, he parked the car and came over to the passenger side and opened the door and extended his hand and helped me out of the car! My legs were shaking as we climbed the steps and went inside of his home! Upon sharing pleasantries, I gave him my musical cassette tape to play through his system as I prepared to show off my singing talents. I wanted to lay down some vocal tracks to the music on the tape and use it to get music gigs and studio work around town! Moses said that he was so sorry that he accidentally erased my music tape and that he would get his guys together and set up recording sessions just for me! I was so happy to hear his wonderful news! However, I was still hurt by his actions and wondered if he erased my tape on purpose?

CLUB OF LEGENDS
TASTING HOLLYWOOD BY MARY LAWRENCE
PART 2

I hear the thunder billowing in the gusty winds and see the lightening splashing across the skies as I peer through the frosty window in a panic of child like fear, and hope for redemptive sentiment of unrequited love! Tossing and tumbling in a restless uproar of haunting emotions, trying to rid myself of the slivers of pain and silent tears that torcher my heart!

I threw myself into a strong and vigorous rehearsal! Singing so many oldy goldy greats from the likes of Aretha Franklin, Diana Ross, Nora

Jones, James Brown; This is a man's world, Ben King, stand by me, a host of Whitney Houston hits, Bobby Byrd and Celine Dion! I sang every word with deep feelings until I was wet with sweat and completely drained! Twisting and twirling, swinging and swaying to the funky beats of priceless melodies, just made me explode on the dance floor like a what? Like a what? Like a sex machine goddess!!

Coming up for air, I noticed that it was 12:30 in the morning! I was in awe at how quickly time had elapsed since I began this soul studded telethon, about 2 and a half hours! Wow! Winding down, I turned off the music and proceeded to the living room for a little rest and relaxation before pouring this aching bag of bones into bed! I decided to call up an old friend and check in! Tee's brother was just telling him that he needed to cut all those other play girl friends loose and find one good woman with whom he could share the rest of his life! When suddenly the phone rang and he started laughing when heard my voice!

TEE--Somebody out there in the universe trying to tell us something, huh? My brother Was just telling me that I need to find me a good woman!

Mary--Oh really! Well you know how the powers that be love to stir up some magic With little cupid's arrow! You just have to know how to run like hell and get Out of the way!! Ha! Ha! Ha!

TEE--You can't run forever girl! I'll be right here, waiting on you!!

We both shared a few laughs down memory lane! I told him I was going to escape those lonely night blues by setting sail on the soft clouds of dreamland!

As I drifted off to sleep, I landed in a strange and inexplicable time and place! Snow flakes were dancing in the air as the fierce winds blew like old man winter's breath upon my cold, shivering body! I was standing in front of an old building with flashing blue and white neon lights that red, Club Of Legends! Instantly, the big wooden and metal door opened and a bodiless arm motioned for me to come inside! Slowly I drug my feet through the door and saw a long serving bar that stretched from side of the club to the other side! There were red, yellow, green and blue lights hanging from the ceiling, with Chinese paper decorations dangling on pretty strings also. The delicate perfume of a thousand rose petals lingered in my nostrils! Glancing about the bar, I noticed some of the greatest famous entertainers, musicians, singers lined the area with drinks in hand! They were a balling and lively bunch, performing some of the most extraordinary live shows that I have ever seen in my entire life! Wow! What a memory! There was Bing and all the old Hollywood gang, Humphrey Bogart, Ida Lupino, Betty Davis, Rita Hayworth, Rock Hudson, Elizabeth Taylor, Louis Jorden, Lena Horne, Elvis, Whitney, Michael J, Patsy Cline, Barry White, Luther and Tupac!

They told me that they had heard me singing and wanted me to join them in their never ending show stopping blitz! They blew their breaths on me and my body flew in mid air to the end of the bar! I was transformed into a glamorous and beautiful Hollywood star, decked out in a sparkling sequined gown that had a long slit on the side, showing off my gorgeous legs and shinning pumps, my ears and neck were covered in precious diamonds and pearls, my hair was long and flowing. The music started to play and I began singing the most lovely melody! I was having a really good time! I felt like I had gone through another dimension!

A mysterious dark shadow body hovered next to me and whispered, it is indeed a great honor to be here, but these great spirits no longer walk among the living! If you stay here, you will surely die! Hurry, we must flee back through the portal of life before it closes and traps your soul here for eternity!!

The body shadow wrapped its form around me and whisked me to a bright tunnel! Looking back, I saw another dark figure lurking behind us with a frozen smile on his distorted, demonic face!! He was commanding me to come back to the Club Of Legends!

DARK SPIRIT--Come daughter, stay here and serve me! You'll be my loyal slave for 940 Years! You must obey! You must obey!!!

MARY--No, I cannot! I screamed. I must live to sing the songs of all the great Legends to future generations!

I saw the evil spirit being snatched back into a prison like cell with steal bars while still ranting in a loud scream of defiance! The other legends, Betty Davis, Ida Lupino, Michael J, Frank Sinatra, James Brown, uttered in unison, she must return to walk among the living and tell the wonderful greatness of our legacies to the world! Let the spring waters flow to a dying world that forgot how to love one another! Sing, children, sing!!!

I woke up grasping and panting for every breath of air! My heart was beating fast like rapid fire from an F16 machine gun! In a blank stare, I fell back unto pillows and balled up into fetal position and hummed a sweet lullabye to calm my nerves!! Wow, what a memory!!!!!!!!

"There are many occurrences in life unexplained by man! Such is a story of greatness! We here at H&W productions feel you should not miss one of the many magical moments in time! Do not deny yourself the pleasure of Mary! Her enchanting, spell-bounding voice and her unique way of presenting her soul stirring and electrifying renditions will overwhelm and astound you to standing ovations! From her upcoming album, called, What's Happening, a question in life, that we too must ask ourselves!!! Come, escape into the world of mind, body and soul! Come, laugh, dance and sing along with Mary!!!!!!!!!!!!!!!!!

With these dynamic captions printed on posters and the Tee Gem label, and also the god father of the underworld, Sweet Black Mosses, formerly of the JBS, I was certain that I had struck gold! In harsh reality, I was about to make a deal with St. Lucifer, himself!!! Without connections to Hollywood and fame, the road to success can be a rocky path of false promises, sexual perversions, drugs and narcotics, emotional break-downs, and even a slow or sudden deaf! It is a dangerous profession, survival depends solely on having a strong mind and willingness to journey on an adventure of a lifetime! Hard work and dedication will yield the desired result of Fame!

The transformation from being a home maker and housewife to being a super star was quite challenging indeed!! As a housewife, I had no identity and was not allowed to have my own opinion! I cooked the food, cleaned the house, washed the clothes, wiped snotty noses and changed shitty diapers, and nobody ever said thank you! All I got in return for my efforts was a brutal beating and put down by my so called husband who took me for granted!!

Now at least I can say what's on my mind, hold my head up proudly and face the world with a great big beautiful smile! I can be a great actress, dancer and singer and receive a thunderous applause of recognition for an unforgettable performance!! My inward soul is filled with blazing flames and I am ready to--

Burn! I'm doing a very provocative and seductress dance, dripping in sweet decadent waves of motions with my hands and legs! It was powerful yet delicately feminine in nature, like sexy Lolita and Marta Hara vixens!

Moses was a gazing like a crazed animal stalking his prey before the surprise attack! He had the patience of a lone oak tree atop a snow covered mountain, however, his jerking nerves made appear to be a fanatic blood thirsty terrorist! He quickly latched on to me and clipped my wings a bit! He did show me a different side of the entertainment world! If something similar ever occurs again, I'll know to run far, far away from his evil clutches!!

I should have been aware that something was wrong being that he was no longer with the JBS. I believed his departure from the group was drug oriented. I based this assumption on the fact that he approached me with uppers, TACS, LSD and Cocaine! Though I refused his offer, as devious as he was, he slipped a pill in my drink! Looking about the room, everything became dark and blurry! Stumbling over a chair, I landed on the bed! Semi conscious, I heard him talking to a friend. Using profanity Moses diagrammed a variety of sex acts that he was going to try on me!

Mary- Oh no! I gotta get away from here! Remembering him tossing the keys on the dresser, I fought desperately to get to my feet! Slowly, I dragged my weakened body across the bed and pulled up onto the dresser. Objects faded in and out of focus, I reached for the keys and they vanished! Wait a minute! Please dear God Help me! Once my vision returned, I grasp the keys, and stumbled to the bedroom window! It took all my strength to push open a passage wide enough for me to squeeze through! Before crawling out the window, I looked back to see if Moses had returned to the bedroom, I could hear his foot steps become louder and louder as he burst through the door! I felt like a ballerina in slow motion seeking my great escape from the evil warlord!!!

He began plugging my pussy with his big shoveled dick and teasing my earlobes with his ravenous tongue! I didn't feel human anymore, I was a mechanical fucking machine! The pressure was to much for me! I remember a blinding light flashing before my eyes as he pumped me full of his white oozing confection! An inward voice spoke to me saying, rise daughter, they will harm you no more! The straps broke as I rose to my feet! Moses in drag, was papered to the wall like fly paper! Get the keys and go to the car, the voice commanded!

Then the voice called the heathens by name! Moses, your mouth is full of lies, taste the bitter fruit of them now! His mouth filled with hot bitter liquid that smelled of dead rotten flesh! You flavored drag queen, you want to be a woman, fill the pain of giving birth! With an awful belly ache, his stomach began to swell! The sniveling cowards whimpered like sick dogs as they were tossed about the room!

I made my way to my car and furthered secured my safety by locking the doors behind me and driving to the nearest phone!

Resting at my Aunt's house in Atlanta, I tried to make some sense out of what had happened to me! I lost all hopes in making it big in Hollywood! Later on I realized that I have learned a valuable lesson! One cannot enter show business with some school girl notion that every accomplishment toward stardom is given on a silver platter, it has to be earned! Now I understand the statement often quoted by Holly Wood Stars "I've paid my dues!" Ones has to start at the bottom and work his way up to the top! Every step I make that brings me closer to my goal of becoming a super star, I will cherish them all with great love and admiration!

Come and go with me if you will, to big cities and bright lights! Look out world, cause here I come!!!!!!!!!!!!!!!!!!!!!!!!!!

THE END